BUT I LOVE HIM

BUT
I LOVE HIM

Protecting

Your Teen Daughter

from Controlling, Abusive

Dating Relationships

Dr. Jill Murray

 ReganBooks
An Imprint of HarperCollinsPublishers

BUT I LOVE HIM. Copyright © 2000 by Dr. Jill Murray.
All rights reserved. Printed in the United States of America.
No part of this book may be used or reproduced in any manner
whatsoever without written permission except in the case of brief
quotations embodied in critical articles and reviews. For information
address HarperCollins Publishers Inc., 10 East 53rd Street, New York,
NY 10022.

HarperCollins books may be purchased for educational, business, or
sales promotional use. For information please write: Special Markets
Department, HarperCollins Publishers Inc., 10 East 53rd Street, New
York, NY 10022.

FIRST EDITION

Printed on acid-free paper

Library of Congress Cataloging-in-Publication Data has been applied
for.

ISBN 0-06-019724-2

00 01 02 03 04 ❖ RRD 10 9 8 7 6 5 4 3 2 1

To Frank, Jennifer, and Michael,

the three most beautiful people in the world.

You make life worth living.

I love you dearly.

Contents

Acknowledgments

THE CINDERELLA STORY that is this book has been driven last by me and first by so many wonderful people.

First and foremost, to the residents of Laura's House, a domestic-violence shelter: There aren't any women in the history books who are more courageous than you. Your strength and desire to give your children better lives has inspired me daily and indeed was the inspiration for this book.

My literary agents, Arielle Ford and Brian Hilliard: You and your staff have been so wonderful to work with. I look forward to many more projects together.

My publisher, Judith Regan, and senior editor Cassie Jones: Words cannot adequately express the gratitude I feel for you. Thank you so much for believing in this book. Because you took a stand here, so many girls and their families will be helped.

My editor, Stephanie Gunning: You are not only a fine editor but also one of the funniest women I know. Working with an obsessive-compulsive writer couldn't have been much of a treat, but you never let on. I will miss our daily phone conversations, faxes, and e-mails. Your commitment to the book, along with the vision we shared, created something truly important.

Dr. Paul Fick, my mentor, a generous friend, and a brilliant therapist: You set all the wheels in motion for me and then stood back, thrilled about each of my accomplishments. I owe so many of them to you.

Myra Gordon, my "sister" and dearest friend: Where would I be today if not for you?

Oprah Winfrey: Because of the invitation you offered me to appear on your show, so many young girls were able to leave their abusive relationships. Your dedication to educating your viewers about domestic violence is more than commendable. You change lives every day.

Dr. Nicki Pike, my guide on so many travels: Thank you for your humor in dark times and the wisdom and clarity that lifted so many veils.

Dr. Raylene Goltra, the sweetest woman alive, with the unwavering strength that I hope to emulate: Thank you for your unconditional love.

Dr. Donald Rowen, a most lovely man with a kind and open heart.

The staff and faculty at American Behavioral Studies Institute: Your love, support, and pride in me kept me going through tragedy and triumph.

Andrea Fox: You are so much more than a mother-in-law but also a wonderful friend. I feel so blessed to have you in my life.

To the three angels who make my life worthwhile:

My husband, Dr. Frank Murray III: Your devotion to me as a woman, wife, therapist, and best friend inspires everything I do. I love you.

My twins, Jennifer and Michael: Thank you for the gift you have given me; to wake up each morning and go to sleep at night knowing that I am the mother of two such extraordinary human beings made this book possible.

BUT I LOVE HIM

Introduction

Our Daughters Are in Danger

THE IDEA for this book came from my experience as a therapist at Laura's House, a battered women and children's shelter in Southern California. In treating more than two hundred women over a two-year period, I found that virtually all of them began their abusive dating relationships while in high school. Many of my clients were hardly older than children themselves: eighteen to twenty-two, some with two children and another on the way. Many had had children with more than one abuser. Many had been kicked in their pregnant stomachs, choked, and punched in the face, and arrived at the shelter with cracked ribs, a broken jaw, or clumps of hair pulled out. Most were bright young women who had had promising futures before they became involved with their abusers. By the time they arrived at the shelter, they were just tired and beaten down, both physically and emotionally.

Certain patterns emerged from talking with my clients about their lives. Many were confused about the signs of abuse and at first had considered their husband's or boyfriend's jealousy, possessiveness, control, and isolating behaviors very flattering. Most then went on to involve themselves in more than a dozen such relationships, each evolving in the same way, beginning with verbal and emotional abuse and developing into sexual and physical abuse. These women were Caucasian, African-American, Hispanic, Asian, Middle Eastern, Australian, Canadian, South American, and Western European. One client held two master's degrees from an Ivy League university; another was a Virginia heiress. It really didn't matter what their level of wealth or poverty, education, color, or ethnicity; they all shared the same patterns of abusive relationships.

The therapists and staff at the shelter were able to help some of these women see that they didn't have to live that way anymore. I still hear from several past clients who regularly update me on their personal successes. Others couldn't imagine a life without their abusers and went back for more. In fact, statistically speaking, an abused woman will go back to her abuser seven to nine times before she leaves for good . . . if she isn't dead. Often my clients acquired "nostalgia amnesia" and suddenly couldn't recall all the horrible things their abusers had done, the things that had led them to snatch their kids from their sleep and leave in the middle of the night without so much as a toothbrush. As a therapist, I became determined to get to the roots of the problem before lives reached these crisis proportions and children became involved in the abuse as well.

Armed with the knowledge I'd gained working at the shelter, I began a program in local high schools, educating teenagers about abusive dating relationships. I was bowled over by the response. Teens spoke openly about jealousy being synonymous with love. They told me that to them the word *bitch* was a term of endearment. Boys didn't think that pushing a girl against a wall or grabbing her face or breasts was abusive—it was merely an attention-getting device. I was stunned to find that both genders felt that punching a hole in a wall or window was an acceptable way to release anger. Girls were in tears during my lectures, and both boys and girls stayed after class to discuss their relationships with me.

Word about these lectures spread quickly among educators, and soon I was speaking with high school students across the state of California and hearing the same sorts of comments. I learned that teenage girls are often very unhappy in their relationships and spend a good part of them crying or apologizing to their boyfriends for things they've never done. I also discovered that teen dating abuse has some distinct differences from adult abuse. Very often women with children stay with their abuser because of economic dependence, religious or cultural mores (till death do you part; you made your bed, now lie in it; divorce is a sin), not wanting to break up the family, feeling that the children need a father, and so on. None of these reasons, of course, is meaningful in an abusive teenage relationship.

While the teen years are a time for girls to explore and develop identity, I learned that the messages from their families and society at large don't allow them to do this important work. Family dynamics play a role in the alarming increase in violence among youth. As a result, these girls actually become active participants in the cycle of the problem.

Soon I was fortunate enough to be invited to appear on several national television and radio broadcasts to speak on the subject of abusive teen dating relationships. The response was overwhelming. The day I appeared on *The Oprah Winfrey Show,* the program's Web site was flooded with e-mail. So many parents saw their own daughters in the stories that more than two thousand requested information and help in the first three days after the show. The following is a partial list of the most common questions and comments parents asked me about their daughters' abusive relationships. How many have you asked yourself?

- Why does my daughter stay with this louse?
- Why can't she see what he's doing to her?
- Why does she put up with his behavior when it's obvious that she's unhappy?
- Why can't she see how wonderful she is? She could have any guy.

- She cries so much; why does he makes her feel terrible about herself?
- Is there anything I can do legally to stop this?
- Is it abuse if he just calls her names?
- He doesn't hit her. Is that still abuse?
- How can she say she loves a creep like this?
- What kind of hold does he have over her?
- He's nineteen and she's only fifteen. Isn't there something wrong with that?
- Her father was an alcoholic. Does that have anything to do with it?
- Her father used to beat me up (or yell at me). Is there any connection between that and her abusive relationship?
- I was in the same situation with her father. How can I get her to believe me when I talk to her about this?
- She's had dates with really nice guys. Why does she keep coming back to this jerk?
- I've taken her to counselors, and it doesn't seem to help. I feel hopeless about her leaving this guy.
- She's sure that he'll eventually change. Is that possible, and how long should she wait?
- I know he writes her letters, which she keeps in her room. Is it okay to snoop?
- How do I help her gain some self-esteem and confidence?
- Is this all my fault? What did I do wrong?
- She feels that if she loses him, she'll never have anyone else. How can I help her see that this isn't true?
- This is her third abusive boyfriend. What's wrong with her?
- Everyone always tells her how smart and pretty she is. He tells her just the opposite. Why does she believe him and no one else?
- She's eighteen years old. If I come down too hard on her, will she leave and go live with him?
- I see her throwing her life down the drain for this loser. How can I make her see the truth?

- I can't have my two younger kids seeing this type of behavior. Should I tell her to live somewhere else if she's not going to break up with him?
- I hear the way he talks to her. How come she doesn't see it? And then when he's around us he acts like an angel.
- My husband and I are now fighting with each other over this situation. Why should my marriage suffer?
- Other people tell us that "boys will be boys" and to leave it alone. Are they right?
- How do I know when behavior has crossed the line between the usual kid stuff and abuse?
- I know my daughter and her boyfriend are having sex, and I disapprove. Is there anything I can do about it? Is that abuse?
- I'm so frightened for her safety. What can I do?

You're not alone. This book addresses those questions and issues and gives concrete steps you can take to remove your daughter from a dangerous dating relationship and ensure that it will not happen again.

The title of this book, *But I Love Him,* speaks to both the issue of denial in the face of logic and the concept of love as a behavior. The fact that you are reading this book indicates that you either suspect or know your daughter is in trouble. If this is true, you desperately want to help her before her life becomes like those in the battered women's shelter, but perhaps you haven't found the right strategy or tools. Like you, I have a teenage daughter, and although I prefer not to imagine her confronting abuse, I hope that if she was, she'd turn to me for support so I could take active measures to help her.

I will attempt to give you not only the hows and whys of abusive teen relationships. I will invite you to look not only at her boyfriend's injurious behaviors and negative influence but also within your family. This book offers an opportunity to increase the level of trust, esteem, communication, and harmony in your home. The greatest benefit you can reap from this book is the ability to create an even stronger family.

Your daughter, you, and your whole family face many challenges. I applaud you for your courage and for drawing on the emotional stamina you will need for dealing with this crisis. I wish you good luck on the journey.

What Is Teen Dating Abuse?

ABUSIVE DATING RELATIONSHIPS and dating violence have increased at alarming rates in the last five years. It is estimated that one in three girls will have an abusive dating experience by the time she graduates from high school. In my professional experience—counseling girls and their parents in this situation—this is a gross underestimation. By this conservative figure, more than eight million girls per year in the United States alone will suffer at the hands of a violent boyfriend before their eighteenth birthdays. Teen abuse is epidemic. In America today, every nine seconds a teenage girl is battered by someone with whom she is in a relationship. What is most alarming is that the signs of potential abuse are also behaviors that young women find most flattering.

I'm sure you never thought you'd be reading a book about teen dating violence. I'm also sure you never imagined that your daughter would be involved in an abusive relationship. Oh, you may have worried about other potential problems: pregnancy, sexually transmitted diseases, and drunk driving. But it probably never entered your consciousness that your own daughter could be involved with a boy who is verbally, emotionally, sexually, or physically abusive. Give yourself a break. No parent wants to think of emotional or physical harm coming to her own child.

The University of Michigan Sexual Assault Prevention and Awareness Center in Ann Arbor defines dating violence as "the intentional use of abusive tactics and physical force in order to obtain and maintain power and control over an intimate partner." There are three key words in this definition. *Intentional* is important to understand because it is clear that your daughter's boyfriend is cruel to her on purpose. As we will discuss further in chapter 6, violence of any sort is a learned behavior and completely voluntary. No one forces a teenage abuser to behave as he does, and it is totally within his power to stop. *Power* and *control* are also crucial words. Like adult batterers, the teen abuser uses tactics of control and coercion to keep his "victim" tied to him.

Before we go any further, I would like you to consider a few questions regarding your daughter's relationship with her boyfriend. If you recognize some of these warning signs in your daughter's relationship and feel that she may be in serious danger, please call your local police or sheriff's department or the National Domestic Violence Hotline at 800-799-SAFE.

IS MY DAUGHTER IN DANGER?

- Before my daughter met her boyfriend, she had more friends than she does now.
- Her grades have declined in the past weeks or months.
- Before she started dating him, she was more outgoing and involved with her family, school activities, and/or place of worship.
- She frequently cries or is very sad.
- If he pages her, she must call him back immediately.
- He told her that he loved her early in their relationship.
- He is jealous if she looks at or speaks casually with another boy.
- He accuses her of behavior she doesn't actually engage in.

- He is aggressive in other areas of his life: he puts his fist through walls or closets, bangs his fist to make a point, or throws things when angry.
- He frequently roughhouses or play-wrestles with her.
- She makes excuses for his poor behavior or says it's her fault.
- They talk on the phone several times a day or for long periods.
- He has a "tragic" home life: he is or was physically abused or verbally demeaned, and/or one or both parents are alcoholics or use drugs.
- He drinks or uses drugs.
- He frequently gives her "advice" about her choice of friends, hairstyle, clothes, or makeup.
- He calls her demeaning names, then laughs and tells her he was only kidding or that she's too sensitive.
- She has become secretive since she started dating him.
- She is miserable whenever she is apart from him.
- She has recently become very critical of her appearance, talents, or abilities.
- She frequently has to explain herself to her boyfriend or often says she's sorry.
- She has bruises she cannot explain or appears nervous about explaining to me.

In the next three chapters we'll discuss each level of violence in detail so that you will clearly understand the problem your daughter is facing and the ways in which you can help her *now*. First, however, consider these statistics on teen dating violence:

- Thirty-six percent of female high school and college students surveyed—more than one in three—said that they had experienced some violence in a dating relationship.
- As many as 50 percent of dating women suffer physical, sexual, emotional, or verbal abuse from their dating partners.

- The majority of violence (as much as 86 percent) occurs during the "steady"/serious phase of a relationship.
- Twenty-five percent of female homicide victims are between fifteen and twenty-four years old.
- One in three women who are killed in the United States are murdered by their boyfriend or husband.
- Results of recent interviews with approximately fourteen hundred students in rural North Dakota indicate that students from abusive households were twenty-five times more prone to dating violence than those from homes without abuse.
- Ninety percent of men in prison come from abusive homes.

These are horrifying facts. The bad news is that unless your daughter wants to get out of her relationship, there is little you can do to convince her that's what's best for her. The good news is that throughout this book we will examine the history of her problem—that is, what led her to an abusive relationship—and the ways in which you can go about extricating your daughter from this nightmare.

The following list, which I've extracted from a project conducted by SAFE House in Michigan, delineates some characteristics that might identify a potential batterer. Show it to your daughter now, and ask her to check off all those qualities that apply to her boyfriend. There is one rule: she is not allowed to make excuses for her yes answers. She is just to answer yes or no. For example, one of the questions involves using a gun to protect himself. She cannot tell you that he bought a gun after his house was robbed so that his mother would feel safer.

- Does he report having been physically or psychologically abused as a child?

- Was his mother battered by his father?
- Has he ever been known to display violence against other people?
- Does he play with guns or use them to protect himself against other people?
- Does he lose his temper frequently and more easily than seems appropriate for the situation?
- Does he commit acts of violence against objects rather than people?
- Does he drink alcohol or use drugs excessively at times?
- Does he display an unusual amount of jealousy when you are not with him? Is he jealous of significant people in your life?
- Does he expect you to spend all your free time with him or keep him informed of your whereabouts?
- Does he become enraged when you don't listen to his advice?
- Does he appear to have a dual personality?
- Is there a sense of overkill in his cruelty or his kindness?
- Do you become frightened when he gets angry with you? Does not making him angry become an important part of your behavior?
- Does he have rigid ideas about what people should do that are determined by sex-role stereotypes?
- Do you have the feeling with him that you are damned if you do and damned if you don't?
- Does he accuse you of:

not trusting or respecting him?
being too emotional, sensitive, or "bitchy"?
lying to him?
being unfaithful or sexually promiscuous?
not understanding him or appreciating him?

- Does he tell you that

all other boys would want you for is your body?
you could not make it without him?

you are "no good in bed"?

no other boy would treat you as well?

no other boy would have you?

you are stupid?

- Are you always blamed for difficulties that arise between you?
- Are you the one who has to apologize all the time?
- Does he show little respect for your time, energy, needs, feelings?
- Does he seem demanding and impatient?
- Is he uncomfortable expressing feelings like fear, anxiety, embarrassment, disappointment, and tenderness?
- Do his moods change rapidly?

If your daughter answers yes to any of these questions, explain to her that it is not normal or acceptable for her boyfriend to treat her this way. In the next several pages we will explore the concept of love as a behavior, and emphasize that none of the behaviors above are signs of love. It will also be helpful for her to understand that while she cannot change any of his behaviors, she does have 100 percent control of changing her own behavior in relation to him. This will be discussed in greater detail.

Remind her once again that love never involves fear or feeling worse, rather than better, about herself. Ever.

WHY IS TEEN DATING VIOLENCE SO COMMON?

According to *Domestic and Dating Violence: An Information and Resource Handbook,* compiled by the Metropolitan King City Council in 1996, there are several factors that contribute to teen dating violence:

Peer approval

Teenagers rely heavily on the approval of their peers. If a girl's friends believe that her relationship is "normal," she is often unable to judge if her boyfriend is displaying abusive behavior.

Gender-role expectations

Although today's teens are being raised in a time of greater equality for women than were their mothers, male domination and female passivity remain prevalent concepts. In high school a girl is expected to have a boyfriend in order to achieve status among her peers. And girls—like women—are generally expected to take responsibility for problem solving in their relationships.

Lack of experience

In general, teens have less experience in dating and relationships than adults and may not understand what is and is not okay. For example, jealousy and possessiveness by the abuser can be seen by the girl as signs of love and devotion. Also, a typical teen relationship is both transient and intense, and a teen's inexperience prevents her from looking at it objectively.

Little contact with adult resources

Teens often feel that adults won't take them seriously and that adult interventions may result in a loss of trust or independence, according to Nancy Worcester in "A More Hidden Crime: Adolescent Battered Women" (*The Network News,* July/August 1993). This is one reason that teens keep this secret to themselves.

Less access to societal resources

Children under eighteen have less access to medical attention and battered women's shelters. They may need parental consent but are afraid to seek it.

Legal issues

Legal opportunities may be different and less available to teenagers than adults. Teens generally have less access to courts and police assistance. These are barriers for teens who don't want to involve their parents in handling the abusive relationship.

Substance abuse

While substance abuse is not the cause of dating violence, it may increase the chances and severity of abuse. Alcohol and drugs reduce the ability to demonstrate self-control and good decision-making skills, on the part of girls as well as boys.

SOME FUNDAMENTAL TRUTHS

Before we go further, let's examine a few key concepts. These are the fundamentals of the therapeutic work I do with girls and families struggling with this type of crisis. They are integral to the abusive situation your daughter is facing and are the best principles I have found to steer your course as you attempt to help her. I will return to them over and over throughout this book.

Your daughter is in denial

She doesn't want to look at her situation the way it really is. She has a fantasy that her boyfriend is going to change, that she is the person who can rescue him, that it's really not that bad, and so on. She minimizes the severity of the problem and makes excuses for his behavior (he's under a lot of stress because his parents are on his back, all of his teachers hate him, his boss is giving him a hard time, he broke a fingernail). She may give herself a time limit for her suffering (after final exams, after the winter formal, as soon as school is out, if he cheats on me one more time). It is important that you do not join her in her denial.

Each person has free will

We must recognize that we all possess free will to do as we please in almost any situation. Armed with that knowledge, we must then accept that with free will comes consequences for our actions. We hope that all our decisions will bring good consequences, but when they don't, we have to take full responsibility for our behavior, because no one *forced* us to behave the way we did. This is true for both teenagers and adults.

Your daughter is an active participant in her abusive relationship

This fact may be difficult for you to hear, but by accepting that she has free will, you now understand that she has made a clear decision to be in her relationship and also whether or not to stay in it. Her judgment may be clouded, but it is still her decision. Likely, you are not the first person to advise her to leave. After weighing all the evidence, she has chosen to remain with her boyfriend.

Your daughter is not a victim

By agreeing that your daughter has free will and has chosen to stay with her abusive boyfriend, you can now clearly understand that she cannot be a victim. Because your daughter internalizes what you think about her, you do not want to give her the message that you feel she is being victimized by her boyfriend. Instead, why not give her the message that she is strong, powerful, and able to make good decisions? There aren't any successful victims in history that I can recall. Some historic figures may have started out as victims, but they empowered themselves to become victorious.

Think about your heroes. Are they victims? One of my heroes is Rosa Parks, who refused to sit in the back of the bus in the segregated South. One may see her as a victim, and indeed, it would have been very easy for her to see herself that way as well. However, there isn't a victim alive who would have taken the courageous stand that she did at that time. You want your daughter to be a Rosa Parks.

All people have control over three things: their own thoughts, their own behaviors, and their own reactions

Your daughter has 100 percent control of these things, her boyfriend has 100 percent control of these things, and you have 100 percent control of these things. No one can control another person, but they can have total control of themselves in the way they think, act, and react. If your daughter has given up her power to her boyfriend, she has done so willingly. By the same token, you cannot have control of your daughter—unless she allows it—but you can have control over the way in which you deal with her problem.

Love is a behavior

This is the most critical point I can make. Love is not what a person says but how he acts. This applies not to romantic relationships exclusively but to every interpersonal relationship in your life and your daughter's: parent/child, teacher/student, employer/employee, siblings, female friends, male friends, and so on.

After your daughter's boyfriend treats her cruelly, he undoubtedly tells her later that he's sorry, he loves her, and he'll never do it again. He tells her whatever has worked in the past. As you speak with your daughter about the tangible actions her boyfriend has taken against her, you can ask her, "Is that loving behavior?" Likewise, when I ask you to examine your own family history, I will ask you the same question.

You can ask your daughter the following questions to counteract her arguments:

- Do you think fear should be a part of a loving relationship?
- Do you think it's normal that a girl in a good relationship should spend so much time crying?
- Why do you need to let him know where you are all the time?

- Why is it all right for him to call you names and make you feel bad about yourself?
- Are any of these *loving behaviors?*

You see, this is another instance when your daughter's understanding that love is a behavior can shut down her faulty reasoning. She will have nowhere to go with those questions, and perhaps you will have given her the opportunity to reassess her part in the relationship.

If she is still in denial, you can ask her, "Why do you stay?" When she comes up with the excuse that at times he is nice, you can reply with my favorite response to abused women: "If you had a daughter, would you be thrilled if she wanted to date or marry a man just like him? Would you think she had made the finest choice possible? If not, what would you say to her? If you raised a son who turned out just like him, would you think you had done the best job possible as a mother? If he's not good enough for your daughter or to be your son, why should he be good enough for you?" That usually shuts down their denial in a hurry.

It is not possible for love and fear to coexist. It is not possible for love and immense sadness to coexist. When a partner displays loving behavior, his mate feels joyous, carefree, energized. She feels like she can accomplish anything to which she puts her mind. If your daughter's relationship includes fear, sadness, decreased energy, and low self-esteem, that does not point toward loving behavior.

Many parents and teenage girls are confused about what actually constitutes abuse, and because the label is associated with scary pictures of severe battering, they tend to discount other common forms of abuse. In the next three chapters I will describe three categories of abuse that teenage girls experience so that you can recognize them. First, let me introduce you to Heather, a former client of mine. Although she may appear to be tough and not at all like your daughter, I encourage you to look below her shocking superficial display.

Heather's Story

At seventeen, Heather was a tough girl who wore a lot of black makeup around her eyes and black nail polish. The high school clique to which she belonged was known as the "gothics." Similar groups exist on many campuses. They are distinguished by their all-black clothing—often black overcoats—and dyed black hair with black makeup. They enjoy looking different from the rest of the kids by all looking the same as one another.

Heather was rude to her parents, lied to them, had committed a couple of petty thefts, and was using drugs. Her parents believed that whatever they were trying wasn't working and feared for her future if she didn't get inpatient help.

Heather was used to being greeted by stares of alarm and disgust, so I pretended not to notice her unusual presentation. It appeared that she wanted me to comment on it, as she frequently displayed her fingernails in some way and ran her fingers through her jet-black hair.

"With your mannerisms, it seems you want me to notice something about you. What is that?" I asked.

"Like you don't see it," she snapped back.

"See what?" I said casually. "I'd rather that you just be direct with me if there's something you want to say or you want me to know. I'm not a mind reader, and I'm interested in anything that's important to you."

"Do you like my clothes, makeup, and all that?" she asked.

"No, not particularly. Is it important that I like them? I'm just your shrink. I'm not anyone you need to impress. I guess the better question is, 'Do you like them?'"

"Yeah, of course I like them. Why would I wear them if I didn't like them?" she asked, rolling her eyes.

"I don't know. I guess because your mom told me that until about three months ago, you dressed completely differently than you do now. So I was wondering why the change occurred. What was going on in your life at that time?"

"That's when I met Robert. He's my boyfriend and he's a goth. My mother can't stand him," she said, emphasizing the last sentence. "I used to dress like everyone else. You know, get my stupid clothes at the mall with those inane little butterfly barrettes. She loved it when I dressed that way. I'm sure she blames Robert for the way I look now, but I don't care. I like it better."

"What about it do you like the best?" I asked.

"I look different. I stand out. I don't look the same as the rest of the weasels."

"Well, actually you do look identical to all of your friends. So, you started dressing like this when you met Robert? How did that transformation into the new Heather begin?"

"I don't know. He just sort of kept telling me little things about how I dressed and would give pointers, I guess you could say."

"What kind of pointers did he give you?"

"He told me I looked ridiculous in my clothes. He said I looked like a mall rat and should distinguish myself from all the pathetic girls at school if I wanted to hang out with him."

"Were you okay with him talking to you like that?"

"Totally, because he was right. So he went shopping with me and picked out the clothes I have now."

"Did you have anything to say about what clothes he was picking out, or did he just tell you what you should wear?" I asked.

"I didn't say anything because he had all the experience in that department. I wouldn't have known where to go or what to get. He also took me to the pharmacy and picked out this hair dye I have now. It's great, don't you think?"

"Well, it certainly is black. What color is your hair naturally?"

"Dark blond. I looked so stupid, like a surfette. Totally no credibility at all," she said, sniffing.

"So, you feel like you're more credible now, I take it. What other kinds of advice did Robert give you?"

"I started listening to different music, which I know my parents hate. He's so smart, and he gave me a different perspective on things I never thought about before."

"Like what?"

"The meaning of life and death, mostly. Death can be a really beautiful thing. Life itself is pretty meaningless."

"How does one do death right?" I asked, quite concerned now.

"When it's your choosing. When and how you decide to do it instead of leaving it up to fate or someone else."

"Have you chosen when and how you want to die yet?"

"Yeah, I think Robert and I will just take a big gulp of Ecstasy and have a ride on the way out."

"Have you tried Ecstasy?"

"Of course, everyone has. It's at every party."

At the end of the session I called Heather's mother and told her about my concerns for her daughter. She had made this appointment for Heather because she was frightened of Robert and his control over Heather. She was wise to have done so.

Although it is my duty to keep the confidentiality of my patients, I am also sworn to breach that confidentiality if I deem the person under my care is a danger to herself or others. Heather was a danger to herself, as she was taking a dangerous drug and contemplating suicide as a romantic notion. Less important but still crucial is that she was in a relationship with an emotional abuser. Robert told her what to wear, how to behave, what kind of music to listen to, and even what to think. He had pulled her from her former friends and family into a dangerous world.

I'm not suggesting that all kids who dress black—like gothics—are terrible or in trouble somehow. I have met many such students who are really lovely kids and like this style of dress. Robert was not one of them. No matter what he wore, he still would have been dangerous, because he was an abuser.

Heather wouldn't hear of breaking up with Robert and thought the notion of him as an abuser was funny.

"You're so stupid," she told me. "He's never hit me or even pushed me. I thought you were different from my parents, but you're not."

I tried to explain to her that abuse isn't only physical, but she was resistant. When her parents insisted she break up with Robert, she ran away. Fearing for her safety, they enlisted the help of the police, who quickly found her at a friend's house. When her parents had called there, the girl said that she didn't know where Heather was.

Because of Heather's refusal to break ties with Robert, as well as her talk of suicide and drug use, her parents made the decision to send her to a school out of state for girls with behavioral problems. The school had an extremely strict environment that encouraged accountability for every infraction. It applied consequences for poor behavior and, most important, Heather had daily individual and group counseling. After a nine-month stay, she came home a changed girl and very apologetic for the way she had treated them and herself while with Robert.

2

Verbal and Emotional Abuse

The First Level of Violence

> *I didn't think I was being abused because he wasn't hitting me. I stayed with my boyfriend because I couldn't see anything physical that he was doing wrong to me. I thought the torment I felt must be all in my head. He always told me I was crazy and a drama queen, so I thought I must be.* —LAUREN, FIFTEEN

LAUREN EXPRESSES the most common myth about abusive dating relationships. As a population, we believe that unless someone has bruises, a black eye, or even a broken jaw or ribs, they haven't been abused. I've even heard this from abused women themselves at the battered women's shelter where I worked: "I probably shouldn't be here because he never hit me." "I'm not like all of you because my man didn't slug me like yours did." These statements illustrate the denial that takes place in abusive relationships. If your daughter is in such a relationship, she is also denying the truth and the severity of her problem. Therefore, it is critical that as her parent, you are able to think more objectively. Clearly, it is time to educate ourselves that words and behaviors can be very harmful tools of abuse. My goal in this chapter is to help you understand the dynamics of verbal and emotional abuse, and see why they are so devastating.

In fact, statistics show that before any physical abuse takes place in a relationship, there has almost always been a long history of verbal and emotional violence. While a relationship may exist at this level of violence and go no farther, it is always true that verbal and emotional abuse are the gateway to physical and/or sexual violence.

As we discussed previously, dating violence is all about power and control. No matter what type of abuse a girl is suffering, these are the common denominators. An abuser doesn't always need to raise a fist to obtain power and control over your daughter; often just a menacing look will do the trick.

> *I guess I liked it when he was jealous. He didn't want me to look at any other boys at school and would pick a fight with any guy who talked to me. Whenever I was out with my friends, he left all these messages on my answering machine telling me that he loved me and missed me. I thought it was so sweet—at first.*
>
> —MICHELLE, SEVENTEEN

Verbal and emotional abuse can be the most devastating type of power and control. In this setup, the boy systematically degrades your daughter's feeling of self-worth by calling her names, blaming her for his own faults, making accusations, humiliating her in public, destroying objects that are special to her, telling her she's crazy, and using menacing looks and intimidation. Think about this for a moment: a broken bone can heal and bruises fade, but without positive self-esteem, your daughter is an invalid. When a person, especially one we value highly, degrades our very soul, how long do you think it takes to heal? Sometimes we never do.

What your daughter doesn't realize is that the behaviors that at first may appear sweet can become controlling, leading to a cumulative effect of domination.

Let's look at some common behaviors an emotional abuser will use against your daughter. All these revolve around being jealous, possessive, and controlling. See if you can pick out one, two, or more from the list below.

Name calling

Do any of these sound familiar? "You're fat, ugly, lazy, stupid." "Bitch, whore, cunt." "Nobody else would want you." "I don't know why I put up with you." "I'm the best you're gonna get."

Nauseating stuff, eh? These are the most common insults abusive boys hurl at girls. Often girls put up with hearing this filth thrown at them because they are used to it; they grew up hearing these names in their home and don't know any better. They accept this type of abuse because it reinforces their negative self-esteem. If a person with high self-esteem heard these vicious, violent words, she might say, "If I'm that bad, then why are you with me? What does that say about you?"

We will discuss family dynamics later in this book.

Intimidating looks

When a child grows up in a chaotic environment, such as one that includes alcohol abuse, drugs, anger, or violence, she becomes very adept at anticipating behavior and reading the expressions on her loved ones' faces. It ensures her survival. The same is true with an abusive boyfriend. She becomes so proficient at "reading" him that he doesn't need to say a word to register his disapproval.

> *He had this look that I called the uh-oh look, as in "Uh-oh, I really made him mad this time." He could just give me that look and I'd start to cry.* —KELLY, SEVENTEEN

Use of pagers and cell phones

You can thank technology for a new form of control. Boys frequently give their girlfriends a pager and/or cell phone so that they can remain in constant contact. This enables the boy to check up on the girl as often as he likes. Usually this means that when he pages her, she must call him back within a specified period.

Of course, it doesn't start that way; a boy will tell his girlfriend that he is giving her these gifts so that they can stay in touch and remain close. Sometimes they invent cute little secret codes that only the two of them know, such as, "When I page you and enter the number two, you'll know that I'm thinking of you and I love you." What teenage girl wouldn't think that was special? Every time her pager goes off with a two on it, she feels like the luckiest girl in the world.

Eventually, the boy becomes angry if anyone else pages her, even her parents, because it intrudes on their time together. It also means that for that moment someone else has access to her attention. He wants to know exactly who paged her and why. Boys also think that if they are paying for their girlfriend's cell phone, they have a right to know who's calling.

Make no mistake: I am not against cell phones or pagers if you give them to your daughter or she buys them herself. You are the only people who have the right to check on your daughter's whereabouts and safety.

> When he paged me, I had to call him back within five minutes or he would really be upset. I didn't have my own phone line, so if I was at home when he paged me and a member of my family was using the phone, I'd get hysterical until they got off.
>
> —JAMIE, FIFTEEN

Making a girl wait by the phone

Let's say a boy tells a girl that he'll call her at seven that night. Where is she at six forty-five? Waiting by her phone, just in case he decides to call early. If she has a cordless phone, she drags it around the house so she's sure to hear it and even puts it next to her dinner plate if the family is eating. Where is she at nine-thirty, if he hasn't called? Still sitting by the phone, waiting for him to call. Not talking with her girlfriends, not interacting with her family, not doing her homework because she's too distracted.

If this happens once, it's understandable. But if it happens repeatedly, this is what the boy is thinking: "Ooh, I know just where she is right now. She's sitting around waiting for me."

> *At least twice my boyfriend would tell me he was going to call me at a certain time and to be available then. Then he wouldn't call. I'd wait around all night for his call because I didn't want to disappoint him. Now I realize how ridiculous that was and that I had a choice in what I was doing.* —BRITTANY, SIXTEEN

Using *bitch* as an "endearment"

I hear this at every high school where I lecture, and it infuriates me. The other day as I was walking to a classroom, I encountered two boys talking; one said to the other, "So, do you want to meet here at lunchtime?" The other one said, "Well, I'd really like to, but I told my bitch I'd meet her for lunch."

Girls aren't blameless in this process, either. Another time I saw a boy yell across the quad to his girlfriend, "Hey, bitch!" She squealed with delight! What a compliment.

Let's get this straight: the "endearment" *bitch* isn't popular because kids hear it used in rap songs. It's popular because girls' self-perceptions are so pathetic that they allow themselves to be called the name and don't say anything about it. Their only concern is hanging on to this charmer at any cost. *Bitch* doesn't ever mean anything good. It's not the same as "honey" or "sweetheart." It comes out of jailyard culture and is synonymous with the word *slave*.

In every classroom, I ask the girls if they would rather be called a bitch than their name, and they all answer no. Again, this is a self-esteem issue. If a girl is called a bitch the first time and doesn't put a stop to it, she's just given her permission to be called a bitch for the rest of the relationship—and opened the door for every other kind of abuse. Don't let your daughter tell you different: it still means the same thing it meant when you were a kid.

> *My boyfriend used to call me a bitch, and I used to call him a loser. I thought it was just funny and there wasn't anything*

wrong with it. After a while, I could see that he treated me like a bitch and I thought of him as a loser. I guess we were.

—NELLIE, FOURTEEN

Monopolizing a girl's time

It's so romantic: your daughter's boyfriend just wants to spend all of his time with her. She loves being "smothered." The problem is that soon he is telling her whom she can and cannot see or have conversations with. She gives up her activities and her friends because there isn't enough time to do all that and spend every waking moment with him. Usually, she isn't "allowed" to go out with her friends, but he can do whatever he wants.

> *He said he loved me so much that he couldn't bear to be without me. I loved that. No one had ever said that to me before. After a few weeks, he started telling me who I could spend time with when I wasn't with him.* —JANICE, FOURTEEN

Isolation from family and friends

This goes hand in hand with the time-monopolizing boyfriend. As a parent, you will need to assess how much of your daughter's absence is abuse and how much is her normal teenage act of distancing herself from family. Look at the time she spends with you versus with her boyfriend. Has it drastically changed? Is she more withdrawn? Does she seem secretive? Once a girl gives up everything else in her life to be with her boyfriend, he's all she has. It's a subtle yet effective plan on his part, because then there's very little chance that she'll leave him. Where is she going to go?

> *I built my whole life around him for the last two years. I don't have any friends now because I put my boyfriend ahead of them. My family is disgusted with me and my promises to break up with him. He's all I have.* —MARYELLEN, EIGHTEEN

Making a girl feel insecure

It is said that just before Bobby Darin went onstage to perform, his wife, Sandra Dee, used to whisper to him, "Your toupee isn't on straight." Just a little mind-wiggling jab to make him feel insecure at a crucial moment. This type of behavior is very common in abusive dating relationships. Often a boy will point out a girl's pimple, tell her that her bra is showing, ask her if she's gained weight, say that her hairstyle isn't flattering, and the like. If she calls him on his criticism, he can claim he's only trying to be helpful because he cares about her and wants her to look her very best.

Making a girlfriend feel insecure only points out the boy's lack of self-confidence. If she feels bad about herself and on edge all the time, there's no chance she'll leave him. This ploy works. You know that if you say hello to your daughter in the wrong way, she bursts into tears. Imagine what her boyfriend can do to her self-confidence.

> *Sometimes he'd gently scratch his fingernail on my face. When I asked him what he was doing, he'd tell me that he thought I had food on my face, but it was a zit.* —NATALIE, FIFTEEN

Blaming

Nothing is ever the boy's fault, and his girlfriend "makes" him do awful things. He will also accuse your daughter of behaviors she may not have considered, such as flirting with other boys or having sex with them. In the psychology profession, we call this "projection." He's thought of or done these things himself but projects them onto her. This leaves the girl in a constant state of uneasiness; she never knows what she's going to do wrong, and of course, the rules keep changing.

Also, as keeper of the emotional climate of the relationship, a girl takes it very seriously when her boyfriend tells her that there's something wrong with the relationship and it's all her fault. This responsibility is fostered in your daughter's teen magazines as well as in societal expectations. Look at the cover of any magazine she's reading, such as *Teen, Seventeen,* or *YM.* The cover promises stories such as "How to Make Him Love You," and "Are You a Good Enough Girlfriend? Take Our Quiz and Find Out." Now think of the magazines that boys read. Not a word about emotional responsibility in a relationship. In this type of scenario, she can work endlessly to fix the relationship, but it's never good enough.

> *Dave always told me I wasn't a very good girlfriend, and he could replace me just like that. When I asked him what he wanted me to do, either he'd say that I should just know, if I cared about him, or he'd tell me and when I tried that another time, it was wrong. I never knew what he wanted from me, but whatever I did never seemed to make him happy.*　　　　　　　—AMY, FIFTEEN

Saying "I love you" too soon

This is the all-time great hook for a teenage girl. There's nothing wrong with wanting to hear the words. Almost everyone has the same basic need to be loved, approved of, and validated. It's wonderful to say "I love you" as well. However, when a boy tells your daughter that he loves her after the first date or even a few dates, he's in lust, not in love. She doesn't know that, and so she's swept away by the romance of it all. In her mind it's fate that brought them together.

Let your daughter know that true love takes time to develop through shared experiences and weathering tough times. There is no love at first sight. That only happens in movies such as *Titanic,* and look at what happened to Jack and Rose. Telling your daughter that he loves her very soon in the relationship may be part of the infatuation stage, but you might want to keep an eye on other behaviors listed here. Your daughter may be over the moon, but you have the perspective to see if she is in danger. Chapter 8 outlines the differences between infatuation, mature love, and addictive love.

> *When Ethan told me he thought he was falling in love with me on our first date, I thought it was the most romantic thing I'd ever*

heard. All my girlfriends thought so, too. After that, it all started going downhill. —GRETCHEN, SIXTEEN

Manipulation/making himself look pathetic

This is a big trap for girls who have a bit of the rescuer coursing through their veins. A boy will tell her of his miserable home life, that she's the only one who really understands him, and so on. All she has to do now is love him enough and his life will turn around. Sometimes he'll tell his girlfriend that he'll kill himself if she leaves him. That is the ultimate manipulation. If he has such a desperate life or wants to kill himself, he needs a shrink, not a fifteen-year-old girlfriend.

> *I was afraid to leave him alone. He always seemed so unhappy. He told me lots of times that his dad had a gun and his mom had sleeping pills. He said he'd just as soon die if we ever broke up, that he wouldn't have anything to live for.*
>
> —SUZANNE, SEVENTEEN

Making threats

This may start off subtly with phrases such as "You wouldn't ever think of _____," or "If you ever _____, I'd have to _____." After a while, this kind of behavior escalates to threats against the girl's life, health, safety, family, friends, or pets. Take all threats seriously, even if your daughter does not. In chapter 13 you will find ways to intervene in this kind of situation. With a boyfriend as dangerous as this, legal action may be necessary.

> *My boyfriend used to tell me that if I ever told my parents what was going on in our relationship, he'd have to kill them. At first I was so scared that I was almost paralyzed with fear and did whatever he said. Then I realized that he was only fifteen and my parents were a lot smarter than he was. They called his parents and then a lawyer.* —FATIMA, SIXTEEN

Interrogating

A jealous, possessive, and controlling boyfriend conducts interrogations as if he were a police detective: "Where have you been? Who were you with? What did you do? How many guys were there? Did you talk to any of them? Why didn't you call me right back when I paged you?" Your daughter must be accountable for every moment of her day. Remember that as long as she is living under your roof, you are the only people to whom she is accountable.

> *If I went to the mall with my friends, he wanted to know detail by detail what I did, what stores I went into, and especially if I looked at or talked to any other guys or if they talked to me. I told him that I didn't talk to other guys but that I couldn't help it if a guy walked up to me and said hi. He'd tell me that I must have led the guy on or flirted with him.* —JULIE, SEVENTEEN

Humiliating her in public

Just to keep her on edge, a boyfriend will tell your daughter, while her friends are around, "What were you thinking when you put on those shorts? Who do you think you are? Pamela Anderson? You look like a whale!" Then he'll give her a little kiss on the cheek and tell her how much he loves her and that he was only kidding. The friends laugh nervously, feeling somewhat relieved. Your daughter laughs, too. Then she comes home and cries. Once again he has managed to sabotage her self-esteem, and she doesn't feel she can get out of this relationship even if she wants. Who would want such a fat whale?

> *Dennis told me in front of his friends that my butt was really huge. When he saw that it hurt my feelings, he smiled and gave it a pinch, saying, "There's just more of you to love."*
>
> —RANDI, FIFTEEN

Breaking treasured items

This is a way that a boy can, once again, rob a girl of something that is precious to her. It shows a total lack of respect for what your daughter holds dear and that his boundaries are blurred. He doesn't care about her possessions, and he doesn't care about her feelings. If she cries about his breaking her favorite doll, the one her departed grandmother gave her, he calls her a baby or says that she's crazy because it was only a stupid doll.

> *I had a Mickey Mouse phone that I really loved. My sister bought it for me for Christmas five years ago because she knew how much I loved Disney stuff. He knew what it meant to me and teased me about it. One day when we were having a fight, he threw it on the floor and broke it. When I cried, he just said, "Oh, grow up."*
>
> —VERONICA, SEVENTEEN

If you have seen any signs of these behaviors in your daughter's boyfriend, it is critical that you show her this list. Ask her if she realizes that this is emotional and/or verbal abuse. Ask her why she is allowing this type of behavior to take place. Usually, a girl wants to hold on to a relationship at any cost. Perhaps, like many people, she may not have realized that her boyfriend was abusive. Now that you have pointed this out, she may wish to explain her boyfriend's abuse to him and why it makes her feel uncomfortable. Let her know that she can try that approach, but a boy who feels he can take these types of liberties with a girl will be difficult to change.

The important thing is not to encourage your daughter to change her boyfriend but to help her change herself and her beliefs about what is and is not acceptable in a relationship. Often teenage girls are merely inexperienced and don't know what the role of girlfriend involves. Just as you taught her to ride her first two-wheeler, now is the time to teach her what a good relationship should look like and what she should expect from a boyfriend.

I have included a teen power-and-control wheel and a teen relationship-equality wheel on pages 34 and 35. The power-and-control wheel will give your daughter shorthand information about various abusive behaviors covered thus far. The relationship-equality wheel will help her to identify the type of behaviors in the relationship she deserves and those she is not getting from her boyfriend. Both are easy to read and understand. Now is a good time to sit down with her and discuss these ideas. Ask her what type of relationship she has now. If she admits that many of the behaviors listed here and on the power-and-control wheel fit her current relationship, you can strategize safe ways in which to leave her boyfriend. Remember, this is a team effort, with you as a key player. Chapter 13 will give you precise ideas on how to go about this process. Please don't chide her for her error in judgment. She is still a child, just learning about herself in relationships. Your love and support will show her that you are safe people to come to when she falls.

Daria's Story

Scott and Robyn were a handsome and affluent couple with two daughters: Daria, fifteen, and Katie, twelve. The couple came into my office on a referral from their family doctor. Robyn had been seeing him regularly for six weeks, complaining of headaches and stomach distress. After conducting a number of tests, he found that there wasn't anything physically wrong with her and kindly suggested that perhaps there was some stress in her life she'd like to discuss with a therapist.

As they began to talk, I noticed that they sat very close to each other and held hands throughout the session. I thought that was a good sign that they were ready to work as a team, no matter what the problem was.

"I feel like a crazy person," Robyn began. "I have all these symptoms, and my doctor more or less told me that everything I'm feeling is in my head, but I promise you, I'm not making it up. I feel sick every day."

After assuring her that I believed she had true physical discom-

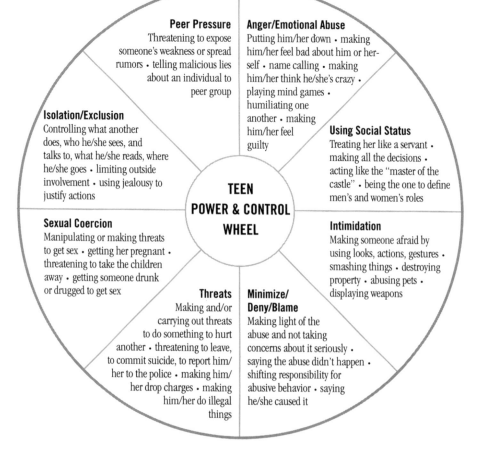

Peer Pressure
Threatening to expose someone's weakness or spread rumors · telling malicious lies about an individual to peer group

Anger/Emotional Abuse
Putting him/her down · making him/her feel bad about him or herself · name calling · making him/her think he/she's crazy · playing mind games · humiliating one another · making him/her feel guilty

Isolation/Exclusion
Controlling what another does, who he/she sees, and talks to, what he/she reads, where he/she goes · limiting outside involvement · using jealousy to justify actions

Using Social Status
Treating her like a servant · making all the decisions · acting like the "master of the castle" · being the one to define men's and women's roles

TEEN POWER & CONTROL WHEEL

Sexual Coercion
Manipulating or making threats to get sex · getting her pregnant · threatening to take the children away · getting someone drunk or drugged to get sex

Intimidation
Making someone afraid by using looks, actions, gestures · smashing things · destroying property · abusing pets · displaying weapons

Threats
Making and/or carrying out threats to do something to hurt another · threatening to leave, to commit suicide, to report him/her to the police · making him/her drop charges · making him/her do illegal things

Minimize/ Deny/Blame
Making light of the abuse and not taking concerns about it seriously · saying the abuse didn't happen · shifting responsibility for abusive behavior · saying he/she caused it

fort, I asked her and her husband if anything different happened in their lives at the time the headaches and stomachaches first began.

"Nothing that I can think of," Scott said. "I was traveling quite a bit that month for my job, but that's nothing new for Robyn and the girls."

Robyn nodded, looked pensive, then burst into tears. "It was when Daria started dating her boyfriend, Davis. He's so horrible to her, you can't believe it."

"Oh, that's right," Scott said. "My wife called me at my hotel one evening and told me she found letters he'd written her. He started

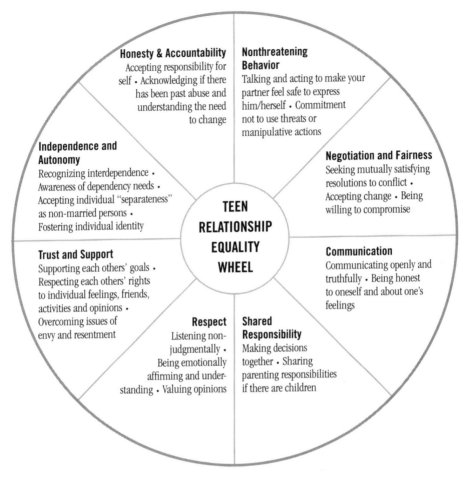

Honesty & Accountability
Accepting responsibility for self • Acknowledging if there has been past abuse and understanding the need to change

Nonthreatening Behavior
Talking and acting to make your partner feel safe to express him/herself • Commitment not to use threats or manipulative actions

Independence and Autonomy
Recognizing interdependence • Awareness of dependency needs • Accepting individual "separateness" as non-married persons • Fostering individual identity

Negotiation and Fairness
Seeking mutually satisfying resolutions to conflict • Accepting change • Being willing to compromise

TEEN RELATIONSHIP EQUALITY WHEEL

Trust and Support
Supporting each others' goals • Respecting each others' rights to individual feelings, friends, activities and opinions • Overcoming issues of envy and resentment

Communication
Communicating openly and truthfully • Being honest to oneself and about one's feelings

Respect
Listening non-judgmentally • Being emotionally affirming and understanding • Valuing opinions

Shared Responsibility
Making decisions together • Sharing parenting responsibilities if there are children

the letter 'Hey Sexy,' and wrote lewd things he wanted to do with her. It was disgusting. She's only fifteen, and we can't stand him."

"You can't believe how my stomach dropped," Robyn said. "I couldn't believe he was addressing my daughter like this. Fifteen years old. Can you believe that? At her age, I was baby-sitting and listening to David Cassidy records. This boy she started dating a couple of months ago is so terrible for her. He plays all these little games with her head. He'll say something little and off-the-cuff about how she looks or what she's wearing. It gets her so upset, she'll cry and cry. She believes everything he tells her. She's a beautiful child."

Robyn took out a picture of Daria and showed it to me. She was precious and looked even younger than fifteen. "What other behaviors have you seen a change in?" I asked.

"I heard him call her a bitch the other day," Scott said. "They drove off before I could say anything, but I talked to her about it that night. She told me I was just being old and everyone talks that way now. She said it didn't mean anything. How can that be? Isn't bitch a terrible thing to call a woman? Am I wrong about this?"

Robyn continued. "She cries more than she used to. As a matter of fact, she always had a pretty sunny disposition, but when she started getting so moody, we figured it was teenage hormones talking. She carries her cordless phone with her all around the house because he tells her he's going to call her. She waits and waits and can't seem to do anything else. The other night we were all going out for ice cream, and she said she couldn't go because Davis was going to call. We told her that he'd leave a message on the answering machine, and she had this look of terror on her face. She said she had to be at home when he called or he'd get mad. Can you believe that? He said that he'd call her an hour and a half before, and now he'd get mad if she went out with her family? Who is he to tell her what to do? But that's the way it is with him. He blames her for all of his problems. If he gets a bad grade on a test, it's her fault. If he misses a shot at basketball practice, it's her fault. It's crazy. I don't understand what she's doing with him."

Scott said, "We talked with her about the letters right away, and she was furious. She felt that we were invading her privacy—and I know that technically we were—but really Robyn was changing her bedsheets and found them under her mattress. We told her that we expected her to break up with him. She had only been seeing him for two weeks when he wrote those letters, and if this was how he was thinking about her then, we couldn't imagine what was going to happen to her in time. She said that he was just being a 'guy' with hormones, and she didn't take it seriously and neither did he. It was just a joke. We felt very uncomfortable about that and decided to keep a closer eye on them."

"Anyway, it's just gotten worse and worse," Robyn said, "and so have my symptoms, I guess. I hadn't put the two of them together, but we are constantly under stress because of this relationship. We've tried to reason with her. He's her first boyfriend. She'll have many others. It's not the end of the world to break up with him. She looks at us as if we're crazy or something. I think he's doing something to her mind. I suppose that sounds paranoid, but really, she's not at all the same. She seems scared and always on edge."

Scott nodded. "She's absolutely right," he said. "We feel like we've reached a dead end, and something is going to happen to her. We've seen his bad behavior to her progress quickly. What else could he do to her? She threatens that she'll run away if we try to break them up. This isn't our daughter. I don't know where he put her, but we want her back."

Scott and Robyn were describing many signs of a verbal and emotional abuser and were right to be concerned. Robyn's symptoms were essentially telling her, "I can't stomach this anymore. It hurts me to even think about this."

At the next session they brought Daria in with them, and right away she glared at them and shut down. Apparently, she thought she was coming to see me to help her mother's illnesses. When we started talking about Davis, she snapped, "There's nothing wrong with him. They just don't like him because they want me to stay this little pink-bowed girl. I'm in high school and I'm allowed to have a boyfriend. They can't take it that I'm not glued at the hip to them anymore."

I brought up the behaviors her parents had mentioned in our previous session and asked her to comment on them.

"It's not like that. They're blowing it out of proportion," she replied.

I knew that it is typical of girls to defend their abusive boyfriend's behaviors. I asked her if he had called her a bitch, and she had said he had, but it didn't mean what I thought. I asked her if she'd rather be called a bitch than honey or babe or even her name. She was silent. I questioned her about her crying episodes, waiting by the phone night after night, not socializing with her family at all, and all the other incidences her parents had told me about. She remained silent.

"Is that all you really expect of yourself, Daria?" I asked. "Don't you believe that you deserve a boyfriend who treats you with love and respect? A boyfriend who tells you that you're the greatest girl in the world, and he's so lucky to have you? A boyfriend who tells you—and all his friends—that you are brilliant and beautiful? Someone who keeps his word to you and calls you kind and loving names? A boyfriend who makes you laugh instead of cry?"

Daria began to cry, and then so did her parents. "But I love him," she sobbed.

"I know you do. But why don't we talk together about what love is and isn't, and what you deserve love to be?" I asked.

Daria came to my office to talk three days a week for three weeks. I felt that since she appeared to be open to looking at her relationship, the technique of "flooding" would be most beneficial. In this approach the therapist does a great deal of treatment in a short time, essentially flooding the brain with information. After each visit, she felt more empowered and confident. I spoke with her in the same manner that you will learn in later chapters of this book. In three of our sessions, she talked about missing her father when he traveled so frequently and feeling pressured to "always act perfectly and set an example" for her younger sister.

Scott and Robyn came with Daria again for three additional therapy sessions, and she told them what she had said to me. Scott looked stricken. "I'm so sorry, honey," he said. "I didn't know it bothered you so much when I was gone. I always felt like you three enjoyed it because it seemed like an all-girls club. Sometimes I feel like I'm out of place in that house. Even the dog is a girl." They all laughed. It was good to see them enjoy one another. Scott promised that he would cut back his travel schedule and spend more time at home, which he was able to do.

Robyn admitted that she probably did expect Daria to show Katie a good example but understood that it must have felt unbearable at times. "Actually, it's our job to raise Katie and show her a good example. Your only job is to grow up and be happy." As the family became more united and Robyn saw the changes in Daria, her physical stress symptoms eased and then disappeared.

Breaking up with Davis was easier than Daria thought it would be. He told her he was getting bored with her anyway. At first that hurt her feelings. Then she told her parents, "I guess a real girlfriend with real feelings and real opinions would be boring to him because he doesn't have any of his own and is not interested in getting them."

3

Sexual Abuse

The Second Level of Violence

THIS IS THE CHAPTER you probably don't want to think about. Being the mother of two teenagers, I can understand that it may make you cringe to think about sex and your daughter in the same sentence. Weren't you just giving her the dreaded 2:00 A.M. feeding, or crying at her first day of kindergarten? However, I must be candid with you. More than sixty percent of high school seniors have had sex before they graduate. Getting the facts about sex can help teens avoid an unwanted pregnancy or, worse, AIDS.

Only 5 percent of American students receive comprehensive sex education in school. This means that the vast majority of teenagers are not adequately informed to make responsible choices about sex. In fact, our daughters and sons receive less than six hours of sex education per year but are exposed to four hours of sexually explicit messages through the media each day.

More than a million teenage girls will become pregnant this year. That is an astounding figure, as is the fact that the United States has one of the highest teen-pregnancy rates in the developed world—twice as high as England, New Zealand, and Canada, three times as high as Sweden, and nine times as high as Denmark. Sixty percent of American teenage pregnancies will end in miscarriage. Of babies born to teenage girls, fewer than 10 percent will be placed in adoptive homes.

Although these facts turn my stomach, and we'd all prefer that our daughter's first sexual experience be later, we must look at our own fears and discomforts surrounding this issue so that we can help—rather than hinder—her ability to stand up for herself in the face of abuse. It is part of our job as parents.

Naturally, abstinence is the best course for your daughter to take. If she is sexually active, the worries and concerns are endless: teen pregnancy, the threat of diseases—one that can take her life and several others that can endanger her fertility—and the emotional consequences of engaging in intercourse before she is emotionally prepared.

Is all sex "abuse"? When we refer to sexual abuse, it is important to remember that all abuse involves power and control. That includes types of sexual abuse that endanger your daughter's emotional well-being as well as more physical forms of sexual abuse. Rape is an act of violence in which a penis is used as the weapon. Other types of sexual abuse, while seemingly less violent, also end with power, control, and domination over your daughter. In most states, children under the age of eighteen cannot legally consent to sexual intercourse.

Date rape and statutory rape are two forms of sexual abuse that all parents can easily recognize as dangerous and abusive behavior.

Date rape

The current material on date rape is alarming. This type of violence accounts for 67 percent of sexual assaults among teens. More than one third of college freshman girls indicate that they have been date-raped at least once. The figure increases for older college students.

In teen-rape research conducted by Suanne Agetorn of the Behavior Research Institute in Boulder, Colorado, it was discovered that of the teens surveyed,

- 56 percent had been raped by a date
- 30 percent had been raped by a friend
- 11 percent had been raped by a boyfriend
- 78 percent did not tell their parents about the rape
- 71 percent told a teenage friend about the rape
- 6 percent reported the incident to the police

Teach your daughter to explain to her boyfriend that at any time during the sexual act, no means no. Often a boy will tell his girlfriend that he "can't stop now," that he's "reached the point of no return." In my lectures, I usually counter this excuse by asking boys, "If your mother or priest walked into the room at that moment, would you be able to stop?" The point of no return is actually just a split second before orgasm. Even a teenage boy has plenty of advance notice so that he can stop.

The difference between "I can't" and "I don't want to" is huge. Girls believe a boy's story about not being able to stop because they don't know any better and are inexperienced. Sex education in schools doesn't teach this fact, so it is up to you to inform your daughter, difficult though it may be. At the moment your daughter's boyfriend refuses to stop intercourse, he is using his power and control over her, and that's called rape.

> We used to kiss and do stuff in his room when my boyfriend's parents were downstairs. I liked it, and I even have to say that I liked it when he touched my body. But the first time we had sex, I definitely wasn't prepared emotionally or in any other way. I told him that I didn't want to yet, but he gave me that stupid line that if I really loved him, I would. I'd heard that as a cliché a million times before, and then there he was saying it to me and I believed it.

He pulled out a condom from his dresser drawer and opened it up. I'd never even seen one before. I felt nauseated. I couldn't believe he was going to do this to me—and with his parents in the house, too. I kept telling him no, but then he kept kissing me and smothering my words.

After that time, I guess he just thought that because he did it once, he could do it any time he liked. It makes me really sad now to know that when I think of my first time, it will be this experience and with him. —KELLY, SIXTEEN

Statutory rape

Even when sex is consensual between teenagers, it can be rape. Different states vary on their age-of-consent laws regarding statutory rape. In most cases the law is stated in one of two ways: either the girl is under the age of fourteen and the boy is twenty-one or older, or there is a ten-year age difference between the boy and girl and one is under eighteen. In both cases, therefore, although your daughter (assuming she is under fourteen) and her boyfriend have each consented, and even if they have used protection, sexual intercourse may still be considered statutory rape. Again, the issue is power and control; the older partner is believed to know better and is expected to protect the younger.

Most states take statutory rape very seriously and prosecute the offender. If convicted, he is legally referred to as a sex offender and may be required to serve jail time, pay a high fine, or attend a year-long sexual offenders' class, or all three. If you disapprove of your daughter's engaging in sexual activity, and her boyfriend is significantly older than she, let her know of the statutory-rape laws in your state. If you are willing to prosecute, ask her if having sex with her boyfriend is worth his going to jail.

Although the following story is not an example of statutory rape, it does exemplify inappropriate sexual contact:

When I was fifteen, I had a twenty-year-old boyfriend. I know that seems like a big age difference—and it is. At the time I thought I

was more mature than your average fifteen-year-old, and he always told me that I was. My parents really disliked him and would always ask me, "What does a twenty-year-old man think he has in common with a young teenager?" But I was in love and didn't listen to them.

The first time my boyfriend asked me to have sex with him, we were in his little compact car. I know it sounds insane, but I thought it was so romantic. He kept telling me that I was beautiful and wonderful, that we would get married when I turned eighteen and have a boy and a girl. He was really persuasive. Of course I wanted to have sex with him. Neither one of us had any birth control, but he assured me that he'd pull out in time, which he didn't. He tried to be gentle, but it hurt anyway, and I kept thinking to myself, "Why does everybody say this is so great?" Well, it didn't last long, anyway.

We continued to see each other for about three months, and most of the time we just had sex. We used to go to the movies and for walks, but he didn't want to do that anymore. He met another girl and broke up with me. Not only was I devastated, but he also left me a nice present: genital warts. —RAMONA, EIGHTEEN

There are two other types of sexual abuse you should be aware of. While they may seem innocuous, don't be fooled. They are sexual abuse nonetheless.

Unwanted touching

Your daughter's body belongs to her. No one has the right to touch it unless there is an agreement beforehand. When I visit high schools, I am always shocked to see the ways boys aggressively touch their girlfriends: grabbing their breasts, cupping their buttocks, and so on. This type of behavior is very disrespectful and treats a girl as if she's a piece of meat.

Once again, many girls take this type of touching as a sign of love. But some girls are uncomfortable even with their boyfriend's arm around them and want their personal space respected. If your daughter is uncomfortable with any type of touching by her boyfriend, it is up to her to say so.

> *He used to paw me all the time, and I felt like a dirty slab of meat. I didn't want to hurt his feelings by telling him that I didn't like it. It seemed to mean a lot to him, and he did it more when his friends were around.* —CATHERINE, SEVENTEEN

Unwanted kissing

Recently I spoke to a class of high school seniors on the subject of abusive dating relationships. There were nineteen girls in the class, and I asked them to raise their hand if they had ever been kissed when they didn't want it. Every girl raised her hand.

Boys usually assume—especially when they are dating a girl—that because they are so fabulous, any girl would want to kiss them at any time. As with other forms of sexual abuse, kissing a girl when it hasn't been invited is another means of domination: taking something that isn't theirs. Our young men must learn that they have to ask permission before they kiss a girl. Even if they have been dating for three months. Of course, I am not referring to an impromptu peck on the cheek, but the type of kissing in which real teenagers engage. Some people don't appreciate or enjoy public displays of affection and prefer to kiss in private.

> *I would get so embarrassed when my boyfriend kissed me at school. But he was so demanding. He'd be like, "Come over here and kiss me, woman." He'd say it in a joking voice because there were other people around. If I didn't go over there and kiss him, I'd hear about it later. I really felt invaded.* —CHLOE, SIXTEEN

Your daughter's boyfriend may physically force sex upon her, or threaten and manipulate her by using other coercive tactics, such as accusations that attack her status as a woman or sexual partner. Following these behaviors, your daughter usually feels worthless, degraded, humiliated, and shamed. Over time, these emotions undermine her ability to escape her abusive relationship. Because she is young and inexperienced, her sense of herself as a sexual being is fragile and her vulnerability is at an all-time high.

I recommend to parents that they take a deep breath and talk to their daughters very openly about sex. Not just the biology course, but about the emotions, risks, and complexities that go with sexual intimacy. You need to discuss such areas as what you determine to be sex: is it intercourse alone, or does it include oral and/or manual sex? If, despite your best efforts, your daughter is going to have sex anyway, will you take her to the family doctor or gynecologist for birth control? Does she know everything she needs to know about the many types of sexually transmitted diseases and how they are spread? Does she understand the proper use of a condom and what it will and will not protect her against?

Just because your daughter acts sophisticated, do not assume that she knows the answers to any of these questions. Without your correct information on these topics—which parents can receive by contacting agencies listed in the Resources chapter—she is most likely getting her information from her friends, who are just as clueless as she is. Do you remember the way you learned about sex? If you found out how babies were made from your friends, no doubt you received erroneous information.

As parents, we must also teach our daughters that they are responsible for the messages they send to boys. While "no always means no" is an absolute, I must tell you that whenever I go to high schools, I see girls who are dressed very provocatively, speaking very sexually, and gyrating against boys. At the moment a girl is checking out his tonsils with her tongue, she needs to understand that her boyfriend's probably not thinking, "Gee, I'd really like to take her to church this Sunday."

I understand that it may be very difficult to talk with your daughter about sex in the manner I've suggested. But you don't have a lot of options. She is not a mind reader, so spell out your values, expectations, and knowledge to her. Don't expect her to follow rules you have *not* set.

If possible, talk with your daughter and her boyfriend together. This may seem mortifying—as much for your daughter as you—but it's the only way he will be certain of your expectations.

I did this with my daughter and her boyfriend. They couldn't look me in the eyes as I spoke and were beet-red during the entire presentation. Afterward, my daughter told me that she had never been more embarrassed in her life and she didn't understand how I could humiliate her like that. My short reply was, "Because I love you and would rather humiliate you than bury you if you contract AIDS. I'd rather humiliate you than see you through an unplanned pregnancy, which would have a lifelong effect on you. I'd rather humiliate you than have you suffer with a sexually transmitted disease that you could have for the rest of your life and that may affect your fertility. Any other questions?"

Although I didn't get the immediate gratification I longed for ("Gee, Mom, you are absolutely right and I promise I will never even think about sex until I am married"), she also didn't growl, snarl, roll her eyes, or tell me I was the worst mother in the world. Her boyfriend seemed a bit uncomfortable around me for a few days, and then he was over it.

Did my little speech influence their behavior? I can't honestly say, but I felt that I had done my job, stated my point of view, and clarified my expectations for them. I am constantly aware, as I am sure you are as well, that one of the most difficult parts of parenting is to actually *be* a parent, rather than a pal. Wouldn't you rather have your daughter hate you for a day as long as she remains safe?

Judy's Story

After I appeared on *The Oprah Winfrey Show,* I received many calls, letters, and e-mails from parents of young teens who were involved in inappropriate sexual situations. One in particular stands out.

A young mother contacted me. She was only thirty-two and had a fourteen-year-old daughter who had a one-year-old son herself. The father of the baby was seventeen and was verbally abusive to this girl, whom I will call Judy. It appears that the pregnancy occurred during a date rape. Judy didn't want to terminate the pregnancy or put the baby up for adoption, despite her mother's protests.

Judy remained with her boyfriend, and the mother believed that perhaps this was the best course to take under the circumstances. She felt—and rightly so—that he should be required to pay child support and that would be easier if he were around. Judy felt that he could be a positive influence in the child's life and the baby deserved a father. Besides, she "loved him," despite the fact that he raped her.

The mother wrote that on several occasions she had heard him call Judy demeaning names, such as "fat whale," "stupid," "bitch," "worthless," and "cow." As the pregnancy progressed and Judy began to show, the school officials suggested that she be home-schooled, as they felt her pregnancy was a poor influence on other students. Judy was becoming increasingly despondent, and their decision sunk her even lower.

Even though Judy's boyfriend made disparaging remarks to her, he continued to have sex with her, although she didn't describe it as consensual to her mother. Because she was already pregnant, he saw no reason for a condom, which resulted in a fourteen-year-old mother with a sexually transmitted disease.

Judy never went back to school because of the humiliation, and she wasn't doing her home-schooling work. She was very depressed and felt hopeless about her life. Most often, she was too overwhelmed to care for her child, so the mother had taken over the task completely. The boyfriend came by once in a while to see his son and played with him too roughly, according to this mother.

Judy continued to have sex with her boyfriend, hoping that he would take a renewed interest in her. This poor mother was at her wit's end and didn't know what to do. She was concerned that if she was too stern, either Judy would leave with the baby or her boyfriend would kidnap the baby.

I advised her to find a lawyer or legal aid to inquire what her rights were as a grandmother, considering that her daughter was a minor and now seemed to be psychologically impaired. I also suggested that she contact a domestic-violence hot line and obtain referrals for therapists in her area who are competent in this field.

At this writing, I have not heard from the mother, nor has she answered my letters inquiring about her daughter's and grandson's well-being.

Physical Abuse

The Third Level of Violence

WHEN MOST PEOPLE think of abuse, they think of physical abuse. As you now understand, there are other types of abuse that are just as—if not more—heinous. In fact, physical abuse is usually the last phase in an abusive dating relationship. Where physical abuse is present, in almost all cases there has been a long history of verbal and emotional abuse and often some sort of sexual abuse as well.

Abusive dating relationships don't begin with physical battery, so it is especially important for you as parents to clearly understand the signs of verbal, emotional, and sexual abuse so that you have a chance to help your daughter before her relationship gets to this very dangerous stage. It is also important for you understand that if you see bruises on your daughter, she has been in a violent dating relationship even longer than you may have realized and has chosen not to leave. If this is the case, please go directly to chapter 13, on interventions. It will help you obtain immediate medical and legal help for your daughter.

Let's be clear about who the perpetrators are: 97 percent of physical abuse is male to female. Many scholars have theorized about why males are generally more violent than females. We have heard reasons such as that boys are raised differently from girls and are given "permission" to be aggressive through the toys they play with. We've also heard the idea that "boys will be boys," which I don't understand at all. Girls are expected to be sweet and dainty— "sugar and spice and everything nice"—while boys are allowed "snakes and snails and puppy dog tails." Is it just me, or does that sound gruesome? Others say it is because little boys are born with testosterone, the "I am man; I will destroy and pillage your village" hormone, and girls are born with estrogen, the "warm, fuzzy, nurturing" hormone, or because men are generally stronger than women. Of course, there is a point to be made about physical violence of women toward men: men hardly ever report abuse, because they are embarrassed. In any case, whether the cause is nature or nurture, boys are hurting girls at an alarming rate.

Let me make this point now, and I'll address it again later when discussing an abuser's thought process: *Abusive behavior is learned. It is not automatic or a reflex. Every time a perpetrator uses violence against his partner, he has always thought about it beforehand and made a clear decision to be abusive. There is never any excuse for violence of any kind—verbal, emotional, sexual, or physical.*

Let's go through some of the most common abusive behaviors that your daughter may experience with her boyfriend.

Hitting, beating, shoving, pushing

This is the type of abuse you can look at and identify; it results in bruises, cuts, broken bones, and the like. Hands are generally used to deliver this sort of punishment. However, a shocking new trend has developed since the "home-run derby" between Mark McGwire and Sammy Sosa in 1998: baseball bats are being used as tools of injury, as are golf clubs, thanks to younger men's new interest in golf. An abuser may feel that if you can use a Louisville Slugger to knock seventy homers out of the park, it can also be used to hit your girlfriend in the head, back, knees, or ribs. An abuser may see a bat or golf club as a weapon of control and violence. Needless to say, injuries sustained with a bat can be extreme.

Pushing a girl up against the wall may not be looked at as abuse, but it definitely is. Shoving her away is another form of physical abuse.

> *My boyfriend used to shove me around and I'd cry. He said to me, "Stop being so dramatic. It's not like I beat you up or anything."*
> —CHRIS, FOURTEEN

Restraining

This is another confusing form of abuse for teens and parents. If your daughter's boyfriend holds her by the upper arms or wrists, inhibiting her exit, it is physical abuse. Many abused girls have handprints on their arms or wrists because their boyfriend didn't let them leave when they felt frightened. What the boy is communicating nonverbally by using this form of abuse is, "You're not going anywhere until I say so. The fact that you're scared and want to leave doesn't matter to me."

Sometimes I'll see a boy with his arm around his girlfriend's shoulder. It is not casually draped, but clutching. While other teens may look at this cozy scene and think it's sweet, I fear that the girl is being restrained and is not allowed to leave.

> *My boyfriend always held my hand just a little too tight. When I told him it hurt, he'd tell me that he didn't want me to get away. The first couple of times he did that, I kind of thought it was cute, but you know what? It really began to bruise my hand and I felt like I couldn't escape his grip.* —SAMANTHA, SIXTEEN

Roughhousing/play wrestling

This is a gray area for teens. Many girls talk of wrestling around with their boyfriends and "play hitting." Many times the boy's intent is to be sexual without permission. He usually touches her in areas he wouldn't get away with otherwise. He may lie on top of her, pinning her down and not allowing her to leave. The boyfriend is reminding her of his dominance and that, once again, she can't get away until he allows it.

> *He liked to wrestle and tickle me until it was painful and I begged him to stop, which he wouldn't do right away. I never said anything, but it didn't ever feel good and I never had fun with it.*
>
> —REBECCA, SEVENTEEN

It is widely accepted by those researching domestic violence—of which dating violence is a subhead—that there are certain undeniable possible effects of physical abuse on women and girls:

- death by suicide
- death by homicide
- disabling injuries
- depression
- difficulty in obtaining, maintaining, and adjusting to employment
- emotional abuse and deprivation
- social isolation by the abuser
- escalation of violence
- loss of self-esteem
- sense of hopelessness and powerlessness
- sense of shame and guilt
- sense of loss of identity
- undermining of a sense of sanity and competence
- breakdown of coping skills
- high risk for alcoholism and drug use

If you see any suspicious bruises, cuts, or bumps on your daughter, it is imperative that you confront her immediately. Physical abuse begins with mild pushing or restraining so that her boyfriend can assess what she will allow him to get away with. By the time you see physical evidence, the abuse has reached a danger state, and your daughter's boyfriend has no boundaries or limits on his behavior.

Adult male abusers have had years of practice, so they are adept at hitting their partner in places where others won't see evidence: the chest, stomach, and the top of the thigh. In many cases, teen abusers haven't yet learned that art, and you may see physical signs of abuse on the arms, legs, neck, and face. Do not rely on an abuser's inexperience, however. Remember that he learned this abusive behavior, most likely in his home, and was taught by example the most effective ways to hurt a woman. At fifteen, he may have already mastered his craft.

Anna's Story

Anna was a nineteen-year-old I saw while working at a low-cost counseling center during graduate school. At the time I knew what domestic violence was but didn't have any experience in its treatment. The O. J. Simpson trial was in full force, and the country was just beginning to recognize that a well-known and wealthy man was capable of committing such heinous acts.

Anna came in for therapy because she felt nervous and frightened most of the time and didn't know why. She thought she was going crazy. She was quite withdrawn in our sessions and didn't volunteer information easily. She was attending a nearby community college and lived with a female roommate. Her parents lived in Michigan.

During the first two months she was in therapy, Anna spoke of her boyfriend's verbal abuse, calling her such things as "crazy," "stupid," "demented," and "repulsive." She mentioned this in passing, really, as she told of a conversation they'd had. She was so used to him speaking of her in a cruel manner that she didn't even recognize that he was saying anything terrible. By her demeanor, I could see what these messages had done to her self-image.

It was difficult to convince Anna that name calling was not acceptable in a loving relationship. She didn't see it as name calling;

he was merely pointing out the truth, and she couldn't fault him for that. I tried to understand why she stayed in the relationship when he clearly didn't value her as a partner, but she closed me off.

Soon Anna was coming to therapy with stories of "mild" physical abuse. The first incident was when her boyfriend gave her a "bear hug" that was too hard and went on so long she felt she couldn't breathe. While she began gasping for air, she asked him to let go of her. His reply was, "I was just being affectionate. Most girls would kill to have a guy who likes to hug them. You're just a frigid prune." I thought his use of the word *kill* was disturbing and told her so. She dismissed it.

Shortly after that, she came in with another story of physical abuse. He had "playfully punched" her arm, and she did the same back to him. Out of nowhere, he "cold cocked" her across the face with his fist. It knocked her to the ground. While she lay there, dazed and crying, he looked in his appointment book to check when he told a friend he'd meet him for dinner. To his surprise, it was that evening. After uttering a four-letter word, he said to Anna, still on the floor holding her face, "Why didn't you remind me that I was supposed to meet Steve tonight? You're such a selfish bitch. You just wanted him to get mad at me, didn't you? That way you could have me all to yourself, you demented freak." Then he left.

I pointed out what he had purposefully done to her. I felt that he had initiated the "playful" hitting so that he could actually hit her harder after that. She didn't see it that way and considered it an accident. She also justified the behavior because she had hit him back. In some way she felt it was all right for him to hit her again. She didn't have an excuse for his leaving her on the floor and walking out; however, she had taken the blame for not reminding him of his dinner date with his friend. When she realized that he'd never told her about the intended meeting, she became quiet. I told her that I thought she was in danger because the physical and emotional abuse was escalating and advised her to leave the relationship. Anna didn't think it was necessary.

The third incident came only a few days later. He became angry with her for something she couldn't even recall. He grabbed her upper arms tightly and began to shake her. She screamed and he told her to "shut up." He shook her with such force that they traveled to a wall and her head slammed against it. Through her tears, Anna told me that all she remembered was the frightening look in his eyes and the severe pain in the back of her head. She didn't recall anything after that. When she awoke, she was on the floor and he was gone.

Her pain was so intense that she went to the campus infirmary. She told the doctor that she was running to get the phone in her apartment, wasn't looking where she was going, and ran into a wall backward. He didn't believe her story and upon examination found bruising on the tops of her arms. He asked her if she'd like to revise her story, and she declined. He asked her the name of her boyfriend, but she wouldn't tell him. The doctor told her that he believed she was in a situation of domestic violence and needed to get out.

She came to the counseling center the next day for our scheduled appointment. I implored her to leave the relationship. I gave her telephone numbers of domestic-violence shelters and information about filing a police report against her boyfriend. I asked her to recognize what he was doing to her and the danger she was in. She became angry with me and left.

As a relatively new therapist, I was upset and frustrated. I could see so clearly what I felt her destiny would be, and I'm sure you can as well. It was through this case that I developed my philosophy about the things we do and do not have control over. I certainly had no control over her thoughts about her abuse, nor did I have any control over her behaviors—or his—in leaving the relationship. I didn't even have control over her reactions to the abuse. That's why I understand your grief and frustration in watching your daughter put herself in emotional and perhaps physical and sexual danger and feeling powerless to help her. I experienced a milder case of that frustration and fear with Anna and many times since in the shelter where I worked.

I never found out what happened to Anna. I called her apartment several times and reached her answering machine. She never returned my calls. Confidentiality forbade me from talking with her roommate or going to the police. In the state of California, a therapist must be quite sure that her client is in "imminent peril" in order to breach the confidentiality of the client. While you and I both know that she was certainly in peril, I could not say that it was imminent. I was stuck.

I hope that Anna is still alive and doing well. I hope that she rid herself of that abusive relationship and decided that she was worthy of something better. Without the knowledge that you have and the loving support you will give your daughter, Anna's future did not look as bright as your daughter's.

Warning Signs

Recognizing Abusive Teenage Relationships

THE FIRST TIME Christina came to my office, she was nervous and apprehensive about discussing her boyfriend and her family. A beautiful and shy sixteen-year-old, she had large brown eyes, and she cried easily. Her long, straight brown hair was parted in the middle and usually hung in her face, making it difficult to see all of her lovely features. Her story is the perfect model to illustrate the warning signs of teen dating abuse.

Following a presentation on abusive dating relationships I conducted in his school, Christina's teacher referred her to me. I recalled seeing Christina in his classroom; she looked down at her desk during the two-hour interactive lecture. She didn't participate in the discussions, and she sat silently as tears ran down her cheeks. I had hoped she would speak with me after class, as many students do, but she didn't. I suspected that she was in some type of abusive relationship, either at home or with a boyfriend, but I was powerless to help her unless she came to me. I was relieved when she called me two weeks later and asked if she could see me. After getting approval from her mother, she came in.

Christina explained that she'd been going with Fernando, an eighteen-year-old senior at her school, for five months. Everything was "wonderful" when they met through a mutual friend. She liked the fact that he was older; she felt protected by him. Fernando took a keen interest in her many school activities, such as marching band and yearbook staff. He also gave her advice about the type of clothes that looked good on her. At last, she thought, I've found a guy who likes to go shopping with me and gives his honest opinion.

Christina felt sorry for Fernando when he told her the types of names his mother called him: lazy, stupid, good-for-nothing, and so on. His father, who had been in and out of Fernando's life since his parents' separation six years earlier, was usually drunk when he saw him, just as he'd been when he lived at home. Sometimes Fernando drank with his father to keep him company.

Christina took it upon herself to fix all the misery that seemed to be bottled up in Fernando's heart. She decided that she would show him how wonderful he was and that his parents were wrong about him. She considered compassion to be her greatest asset.

Like her boyfriend, Christina came from a second-generation Hispanic family, although her mother was Caucasian. Her father only had a sixth-grade education, but he worked hard for the family as a laborer. Her mother had an associate's degree from a junior college and worked as a legal secretary.

Sure, her parents fought, but didn't all parents? Not that it didn't upset Christina and her four younger siblings to hear the arguments, but usually the fighting was done late at night, when the little ones were asleep. Christina came out of her room once to witness her father backhand her mother across the face and spit on her when she cowered on the floor. She tried to come between them, but her father pushed her away, and her mother cried out, "I'm fine. Go back to your room." Christina ran away, terrified, hearing her father call his wife a "whore and a bitch that thinks she's better than anyone else." A moment later the door slammed, and she heard her mother crying.

The next morning her mother had a bruise on her face that she attempted to cover with makeup. Christina asked where her father was and was told that he got a call from his supervisor to come into work early. Christina knew it was a lie, because her mother didn't look her in the eyes when she said it. Her little brothers and sisters were very quiet that morning.

Christina's parents fought like that at least once a week. Everyone in her father's family called her mother a "saint" because she "stuck it out with him" like a "good girl" is supposed to do. They said, "When you make a vow before God, you do not break it." Christina loved her father and didn't understand why he treated her mother like that. She worked so hard. Even when her father was out of work, her mother stayed at her office, working overtime and weekends to help make ends meet. Sometimes they were affectionate with each other, especially after a fight, when her father brought home candy and oranges. But her mother still seemed cautious, and flinched just a little when he put his arm around her.

So Christina knew all about Fernando's pain, having experienced quite a bit herself. She was certain that she could be the one to help him. He told her he was falling in love with her after their second date, and that was like music to her ears. She had waited her whole life to be swept away by a knight on a horse, and here he was. She couldn't believe how lucky she was. She was sure that her love for him would fix his dismal life.

Fernando loved Christina so much that he wanted to see her every school day at lunchtime and in the evenings as well. Although she'd had a group of girlfriends she usually ate with, they didn't mind his joining their lunch bunch. All of her friends told her how special he was and admired the way he looked at her with affection. Sometimes he would brush her hair out of her face and tell her he wanted to see how beautiful she was. If other boys looked in Christina's direction, he shot them a dirty look or even went up to them, asking, "Are you looking at my girl?" Christina's friends let out a collective sigh.

After a couple of weeks, Fernando told Christina that he wanted to eat lunch with her alone, and although she felt bad for her friends, she agreed. The girls were a little taken aback. After all, they had known one another since elementary school. But they thought it was terribly romantic that he wanted to spend all that time alone with her. It was so *Romeo and Juliet.*

In the beginning of their relationship, Fernando came to every one of Christina's band practices. At break time, he often inquired about some of the boys in the band and their intentions toward her. She thought it was so sweet the way he was just a little jealous and needed her reassurance. She believed he truly loved her at those moments, so she went out of her way not to talk with the other boys in the band, even though they had been good friends before. It was important to Fernando that he knew she was his and his alone. With all the misery he faced at home, Christina felt that was the least she could do.

Fernando acted the same way with the boys on the yearbook committee. He came by after school when Christina worked on a yearbook project and gave the guys a dirty look. He never came into the yearbook office; he'd just hang around outside until she was finished. Just knowing the way he loved her somehow made her parents' fights at home more bearable.

Fernando and Christina spoke on the phone every night for at least an hour. The time demands made it difficult for her to finish her homework in the evening, so she started waking up an hour earlier to get everything done. Fernando did poorly in school. She knew he was smart and could do better, but she decided that the stress of his home life didn't allow him to excel the way she knew he could. Sometimes she'd write an English paper for him or help him with a science report. She was an A-minus student and was only too happy to give him some pointers.

After two months of dating Fernando, Christina stopped getting phone calls from her girlfriends. They all seemed to be busy with other friends, but that was okay. Fernando had told her of several occasions when he overheard her friends discussing her in a mean-spirited fashion. Besides, Christina had Fernando and didn't need anyone else.

The only thing she didn't like was when Fernando came to pick her up and she could tell he had been drinking. He was a little surly at those times and said things he didn't mean. Sometimes she'd cry, and he would apologize the next day. He could be so sweet when he wanted. Once, after he said ugly things to her, he brought her a little stuffed bear holding a tin of chocolate kisses and told her, "This is how many times a day I think of kissing you." She opened the tin to find two dozen chocolates. Her heart melted.

Fernando suggested having sex with her on their two-month anniversary. Although she was very hesitant and her religion forbade premarital sex, she knew that if she had sex with him, Fernando would really know she was interested in spending her life with him. It wasn't what she had expected: it was always quick, a little rough, and even hurt a bit. She decided that this must be what sex was all about—no wonder her mother complained about it so much as a "woman's duty." Fernando seemed happy with the sex, and that was all that mattered.

Shortly thereafter, Christina quit the yearbook staff because it was taking time away from her relationship with Fernando. He wanted to see her more often. She became more introverted because he insisted that she was always flirting with other guys. She began wearing loose pants more often because he was worried that with her wonderful figure, she might be giving guys the message that she was available. She stopped wearing any makeup for the same reason. Although Fernando's home life remained unpleasant, Christina was certain that he was happier with her.

Christina began getting stomachaches and headaches. Her mother took her to the doctor, who said there was nothing wrong and that it might be stress-related. Her mother laughed and asked him what kind of stress a sixteen-year-old girl could have.

Christina couldn't make it to band practices because Fernando always seemed to be in some sort of crisis during those times. She was forced to quit. She told her parents that practice was interfering with her studies, but when both her math and science teachers called home in the same week to inform them of her poor grades, Christina felt that her world was beginning to crumble. She had set her hopes on a scholarship to UCLA, and her parents had always been very proud of her academic achievement.

Every day Fernando seemed to accuse her of something new: Why was she wearing that outfit? Did she think she was better than he was? Why did she look at another guy? He bought her a pager, and she had to call him back within ten minutes after he paged her. On one occasion she was at the market with her mother and couldn't find a phone. She became so ill with worry that she threw up in the market. Fernando was angry and told her that her not calling back immediately meant that she didn't care about him and was too selfish to put his needs first. Christina also had trouble sleeping because if Fernando was worried in the middle of the night, he paged her. She slept fitfully, not knowing if her pager would go off and awaken her sisters, who shared her bedroom.

When Christina came to see me, she didn't think she needed help, although her teacher and mother did. She told me she came in only to get them off her back. She also said that she loved her boyfriend and was certain that if she just kept him happy, everything would be fine. She didn't understand when I suggested to her that she was in an abusive relationship. "That's ridiculous," she said. "He's never even hit me. I'm nothing like my mother. I'd never allow a man to hit me."

Christina's therapy was slow and painful for her. She was so invested in her abusive relationship that she resisted any insight or suggestions. I gave her a list of abusive behaviors (see pages 8–9) as well as a list of the characteristics of an abuser. I asked her to go home, look at the lists honestly, and check off those items that applied to her relationship and to Fernando. She didn't bring the lists back at her next appointment. She told me that Fernando had a series of crises during the week to which she had to attend. He also told her that I was brainwashing her, and I was probably a lesbian who hated men.

She eventually brought in the lists, not checked, saying that some of the items applied to Fernando and her, but she had an excuse for every one. When she accepted my key principle that love is a behavior, her thinking began to turn around. She was able to see the similarities between her relationship with Fernando and her mother's relationship with her father. We began talking about their marriage as a role model for her, as well as other family, religious, and cultural dynamics.

After four months of weekly counseling, Christina was able to leave Fernando, although she needed a restraining order to keep him away. Shortly thereafter, she saw him with another shy, mousy girl at school. She was pained by the fact that she could be so easily replaced. "So, what you're upset about is that he's your abuser and no one else can have him," I told her. She had to laugh at the ridiculousness of her thought.

Unfortunately, Christina continues to live in an abusive home. Often a mother knows she's being abused but feels powerless to change the situation. If she can prevent her daughter from suffering the same fate, she will do everything she can to help. In Christina's case, her mother had shown her sixteen years of the way in which a woman was expected to behave in such a relationship.

Wisely, Christina decided to take a break from dating and concentrate on her schoolwork. Soon she was up to her usual standards; however, because of the competitiveness of her school of choice, she didn't receive her scholarship, nor did she get accepted as a freshman. The one semester of poor grades had eliminated her opportunities. She decided to enroll at a community college and reapply to UCLA the following year.

Based on the information you've read in chapters 1 through 4, what warning signs could you have told Christina about? Which behaviors did you see in her relationship that are similar to your daughter's and her boyfriend's? There were plenty of warning signs that Christina was in an abusive relationship:

He called her names and said ugly things about her "that he really didn't mean."

He bought her a pager and expected her to call him back within ten minutes.

He monopolized all her time. She was with him at school during lunch, after school, and on the telephone—even in the middle of the night.

He isolated her from family and friends. She lost all her friends because of her relationship. He lied to her about her friends' betrayal, and she didn't question it. After her breakup, she confronted her friends. They had never said any of the things of which they were accused.

He made her feel insecure. He pointed out her imperfections as a way of "helping her."

He blamed her, accusing her of wearing provocative clothing, being interested in other boys, wearing makeup to attract other boys, and so on.

He was possessive. He needed to know where she was at all times and constantly checked up on her through phone calls and her pager.

He was jealous. Shortly after they met, he began confronting boys who even glanced in her direction.

He said "I love you" too soon—on their second date. How much did they really know about each other?

He made himself look pathetic. She needed to rescue him all the time, any hour of the day. She wasn't even allowed to sleep. In fact, Fernando never brought Christina to his home—with the excuse that he was embarrassed by his mother's behavior—and she still doesn't know if the stories he told her were true.

He used alcohol. He drank to "keep his father company while he drank." She soon realized that he drank more often than he claimed to see his father.

He coerced her sexually. Although it was Christina's responsibility to tell Fernando she didn't want sex, he asked for it too soon, was rough with her, and didn't care about her feelings.

Christina's story reveals why it is important that your daughter understand that love is a behavior. It is your job to teach her. At almost any time during her relationship, her mother could have asked her, "Is that loving behavior? You say that you love him, so would you do these things to him? Why is it okay for him to do these things to you?" Understanding that concept could instantly break down your daughter's defenses and, indeed, her arguments and excuses for her boyfriend's unacceptable behavior.

In addition, if Christina had understood that she has control over only three things—her own thoughts, her own actions, and her own reactions—she would have understood that she couldn't "save" Fernando. She would have realized that she could not change his behavior, although she could control her actions regarding his behavior (leaving him, or at the very least, standing up for herself). She also had 100 percent control of her reactions to his behavior. What she *chose* to do was make excuses, live in denial, try to appease a boy who kept changing the rules, and stay in the relationship.

Was Christina a victim? In my mind, she was a victim of her upbringing and home life, which taught her that this type of relationship was normal. She was a victim of her mother's decision to keep her in an abusive home environment instead of standing up to her father, getting counseling, or leaving him so that the children were not subjected to violence and fear. We will discuss family dynamics in detail in chapter 10, and as you can see from Christina's story, this is an essential element for predicting future abusive relationships.

I refuse to think of Christina as a victim in her relationship, however. She was crying, she lost her friends, she was "forced" to leave the activities she loved, her grades were suffering, she was aware that her dream of receiving a scholarship to UCLA would remain unrealized. She didn't like the way he spoke to her; she didn't like to be awakened in the middle of the night; sex was painful. Nonetheless, at any moment she could have said, "Enough is enough. I don't deserve to be treated this way." Then she could have left the relationship. Remember, Christina had 100 percent control of her actions.

An abusive relationship can begin innocently, then through small, almost imperceptible behaviors—most of which your daughter finds flattering and romantic—it can turn into a nightmare. Fortunately, things turned out relatively well for Christina. In my private practice and at the schools where I lecture, I constantly hear horrific stories that I'm certain will become even more tragic without intervention. If you have seen your own daughter in Christina's story, why not share this chapter with her? Often teens see themselves more easily through the eyes of a peer.

Now that you've read Christina's story, you must be wondering what Fernando's story is. Why do boys turn into abusers?

6

What's He Thinking?

How to Spot a Potential Abuser

WHEN I WORKED at a battered women's shelter, the first questions the residents usually asked were, Why does he do this? What's wrong with him? Can he change? Did I do something wrong? Is there a chance that we can get back together? I kept telling him that he was hurting our family and me—why didn't he listen? Are we that unimportant to him?

These are all good questions and ones that you and your daughter undoubtedly have posed yourselves. More specifically, what goes through the mind of an abuser, and how did he begin treating women in such a violent manner at a young age? In this chapter I will try to answer all these questions.

Abusive behavior begins in childhood. Almost without exception, teen abusers fit a typical profile:

- They have been physically and/or psychologically abused as children.
- They have seen their father beat and/or severely dominate their mother or sisters.

- One or both of their parents abused, or continue to abuse, alcohol, or use drugs.

I repeat: as parents, it is one of our primary jobs to model the behavior we want our children to take into adulthood. If we hit or spank them, we can expect them to understand that violence is the way to solve problems or get what they want. If we yell at them or use demeaning language, we can expect them to hold in their anger as young children—because they can't fight back—and then display the same language toward others when they are teenagers. If a boy sees his father dominate and intimidate his mother, he understands that this is the way men behave toward women. If he sees his father hit his mother, he understands that physical domination is a man's right in his relationships. If he sees that his mother tolerates this behavior—that is, she doesn't leave or at least stand up for herself—his perception is that women feel this is acceptable behavior. The list goes on, but the concept is clear: children learn what they live.

When I was a kid, my father used to whip me with a belt buckle until I bled. He also smacked my sisters across their faces and called them bitches. He used to tell me that I was good for nothing and would never amount to anything. He would push my mother up against walls and call her a whore. If he didn't like what she cooked for dinner, he'd tell her it tasted like shit and throw it on the floor. She didn't do anything to protect my sisters and me because I know she was scared herself.

I was terrified of my father, and there were lots of times I wished he would get into a car accident on the way home from work. I felt so guilty about it that I would go to confession two or three times a week. Now I wonder why the priest didn't file an anonymous child-abuse report.

I loved my mother, but I didn't respect her at all. I couldn't believe she was keeping us in that house or understand why she didn't have my father arrested. As much as I hated all that, it's exactly what I became when I started going out with girls. I never hit them, but I'd be real mean to them and make them feel bad about themselves. I always made one of my girlfriends cry, and I hated that, because my mom would cry all the time.

One day my oldest sister said to me, "You know what? You're just like dad. You make me sick the way you treat women. How could you do that when it was done to you and you saw it done to us?" I couldn't believe it. She was absolutely right. I had turned into my dad. I was so mad that I started abusing myself by hitting my head against the wall, driving recklessly, and stuff like that. Then I thought, you know, you're just taking up where your father left off. You don't need him to torture you anymore because you do it to yourself. The next day, I went in to see the school psychologist.

—ANDY, NINETEEN

Another characteristic of a potentially abusive boyfriend is one who loses his temper frequently and more easily than most people. He may throw or hit objects rather than people. I am always concerned when I hear of boys who punch holes in their bedroom walls or closets. In many households it is considered acceptable behavior, because parents reason that their son has excess energy when he's upset, and he's not harming anyone. This is poor logic for two reasons. First, while the brain is a magnificent piece of equipment, when a person punches holes in walls, after a short while it cannot discriminate between a wall and a cheekbone or jaw. All the brain knows is that when it hits *through* something, anxiety is relieved and it feels better. It then seeks other destructive opportunities. This is not the same as hitting a punching bag or pillow, which are good aids for deflecting anger since they are not destroyed by the act. Aside from perhaps Evander Holyfield, I doubt anyone can put a hole in a punching bag.

The second reason for my concern about boys who punch their walls is that it hurts, however little they feel the pain in the moment. I believe that punching a wall is similar to self-mutilation—the cutting of one's arms or legs. Self-mutilators—usually girls or women—

are in tremendous psychological pain. When they feel very anxious and the pain is intolerable, they cut themselves because they would rather feel the physical than the psychological pain. When they see blood, it is evidence of their torment. In many cases, they will not even feel the physical pain because there is an anesthetic effect.

Can you see the similarities between the young man who punches a wall and the young woman who cuts herself? We would definitely think that she needs extensive and immediate psychological help, wouldn't we? I don't see a tremendous difference between the two, except that the young woman is only abusing herself, while the young man's behavior can quickly generalize to include your daughter.

> *My boyfriend used to punch his walls all the time. It became a joke because every time he did, he'd say, "I guess I'd better get another poster to cover it up so my parents don't find out." I thought it was a little weird that he did that, but because he made such a joke of it, I wasn't too concerned until he started playfully punching my arm. He's pretty strong, so sometimes it would hurt. I mentioned it once and he said, "Oh, come on. You know I'd never hurt you. I'm only fooling around." When he slammed my head against the wall, I got out. What was I thinking?* —JANINE, SEVENTEEN

Often an abusive boyfriend appears to have a dual personality. Most of the time he is nice and considerate to your daughter. Other times he makes cruel and demeaning comments, becomes enraged when she doesn't listen to his advice, when he doesn't know where she is at all times, or when he uses drugs or alcohol. When an abusive boyfriend expresses remorse and begs for forgiveness, it keeps her in the relationship. She may say, "He's not mean all the time. He can be so sweet." This could certainly be true. No one is 100 percent monster.

Is your daughter constantly blamed for any difficulties that arise between them, or even any difficulties in his life? Abusive boyfriends are very adept at turning their behavior around to blame their girlfriends. This makes her wrong, as if she's disappointing him. She believes that she can't trust her instincts and that she has to apologize for "crimes" she didn't commit. Because she feels like such a "loser," she believes him when he tells her that he is the only boyfriend who would put up with her and she should be happy that he keeps her around. Do you see how insidious this behavior is? This boy does not take responsibility for any of his actions; it is likely therefore that he will not change.

Many abusers have very rigid, stereotyped ideas of male and female roles. An abuser may think that women are inferior to men and believe that a man has the right to discipline his girlfriend physically. He may tell her that God made men superior to women, thereby giving him special privileges. This type of boyfriend believes that your daughter ought to be submissive, dependent, respectful, and quiet; she should "know her place." Although he may not be that blatant in his chauvinism, he may reveal his belief that he is superior to your daughter by using demeaning comments about women in general, or speaking of women as chicks, babes, or broads.

> When the O. J. Simpson trial was happening, I was just a young teenager, but I thought that he was right about a lot of things. I didn't think he should have killed his wife, but I identified very strongly with the description that Nicole's sister gave about one of his comments. It was the one where he grabbed her crotch and said, "This belongs to me." When a woman marries a man, she gives herself to him body and soul. It is not for her to demand things or even think that she is completely equal to him. God made men stronger for a reason. He made women childbearers for a reason. Why should it be up to us to fool with God's plan?
>
> —ZACK, NINETEEN

Substance abuse is as big a problem with many teenage abusers as it is with abusive adult males. Alcohol use among teenage males is now at an all-time high. The use of crystal meth is out of control.

Heroin is making a steady comeback, and marijuana use has risen dramatically. (I will talk about these drugs in greater detail in chapter 9.) What does this mean to your daughter? If her boyfriend abuses drugs—or states that he uses them recreationally (for instance, at a party)—she is in more danger than you may realize. Her boyfriend cannot be expected to make good decisions on behalf of your daughter when his thinking and motor skills are severely impaired. Of course, he thinks he's fine and may become angry when she suggests he not drive her home or if she asks him to give her the keys.

Another important reason that your daughter is in danger is that we are now aware that chronic use of marijuana or crystal meth causes rage and paranoia. Unfortunately, there are no guidelines as to what the term *chronic* means. For one person it may be one joint a day; for another, it may be one joint every three days over a sustained period. You can certainly understand the ways that rage and paranoid delusions on the part of her boyfriend could jeopardize your daughter's safety. He can easily use his substance abuse as a convenient excuse to be violent toward her. It is also true that people who use drugs or alcohol do so to avoid problems.

We now know scientifically that the age at which a person begins using drugs or alcohol steadily is the emotional age at which they remain, unless serious rehabilitation is undertaken. Please see chapter 9 for a further discussion.

> *When I smoked weed, I felt like my mind was quiet and peaceful. It was a great feeling. My home was terrible, and the only way I thought I could escape was to smoke and get rid of the bad feelings. I started doing it when I was thirteen, and I knew I couldn't leave my house for a few years. It was the only way I thought I could survive.*
>
> *When I was fifteen, I got a girlfriend. She didn't like me to smoke because she said it made me weird. I thought she should just get off my back because she couldn't imagine what my life was like. By this time, I was smoking about five joints a day, and*

I always felt mad at her. I'd accuse her of being just like my mom and trying to control me.

One day I couldn't stand it anymore and whacked her across the face. I don't even know what possessed me to do that. Her parents called the police, and I was in lockup for two weeks. I think the judge was just trying to make an example of me. I went through bad withdrawal in there, and my counselor got me to understand how addicted I was and the price I was already paying because of it. My future looked even worse if I didn't stop, so I did.
—DOUG, SEVENTEEN

The following are some important concepts for you to understand about abusive boyfriends. I hope you will share them with your daughter.

- Abuse is a learned behavior. It is learned from seeing it used as an effective tool of control—usually in the home in which he grew up.
- Abuse is not a natural reaction to an outside event.
- It is not normal to behave in a violent manner within a personal relationship.
- Abusers deny that abuse has occurred or make light of a violent episode.
- Abusers blame the victim, other people, or outside events for the violent attack.
- Abusers don't act because they are out of control. They choose to respond to a situation violently. They are making a conscious decision to behave in a violent manner.
- Abusers know what they are doing and what they want from their girlfriend.
- Abusers are acting not out of anger but out of their need for control and domination.
- Abusive boyfriends are not reacting to stress.
- Abusers are not helplessly under the control of drugs or alcohol. They make a decision to drink or use drugs.

- Abusive boyfriends may be hard workers and good students.
- Abusers may be so charming and engaging that others would never suspect they are abusive.
- Abusive boyfriends may at times be loving and gentle.

The last three points are especially important to grasp because they refer to situations that can be deceptive; an abuser may appear to be exactly the type of boy you would like your daughter to date. You might even describe him as a "good catch."

As I mentioned, many abusers have something of a dual personality; that is, they are capable of excelling in school and holding down responsible jobs. Does that necessarily preclude them from being violent or inappropriate with your daughter? No.

An abuser also uses his charisma as a ploy to enter a girl's life and keep her parents from being suspicious of him. This type of behavior throws parents off track and often allows them to feel their daughter is so safe with this boy that they don't need to "meddle" or supervise the twosome at all.

As to the last point, as previously stated, abusers aren't monsters 100 percent of the time. The kind-and-loving phase—which may occur after a blowup—is a prime reason girls and women remain in abusive relationships. This is also referred to as the "honeymoon phase." When an abuser is acting sweetly and appears to be truly remorseful for his actions, the girl desperately wants to believe him and therefore sees no point in leaving the relationship. Why should she leave now, when he's being so nice?

Make no mistake: if abuse of any type occurs once in a relationship and it is not addressed, it will continue and may escalate, regardless of whether the boy appears to be Mr. Wonderful.

CAN HE CHANGE?

Your daughter may think her love has the power to change her abusive boyfriend. This is faulty thinking. As I've said, only he can change his behavior, and your daughter has no control over that. This may play into the self-blame she carries, which was originally placed there by her boyfriend: *If I tried harder, he could have changed. If I was good enough, he could have changed.* Once again, let your daughter know that it's not her job; it's her boyfriend's.

Can an abusive boyfriend change his own behavior? The answer is a resounding yes. Abuse is a learned behavior, and it can be unlearned, but only if he chooses to do so. It's just like the old joke, "How many psychologists does it take to change a lightbulb? Only one, but the lightbulb really has to want to change."

A boy can change his abusive behavior if

1. he understands that his behavior is inappropriate and abusive.
2. he doesn't cast blame for his behavior onto his girlfriend, parents, teachers, or anyone else.
3. he takes full responsibility for his abusive behavior.
4. he has a desire to change. He's not just doing it to stay out of trouble at school or with the law or because his girlfriend nagged him to do so.
5. he follows up his stated desire to change with concrete actions. Love is a behavior!
6. his new actions are continuous, not just for the moment. Most abusers apologize for their bad behavior and tell their girlfriend it will never happen again. Often, they are contrite for only a few days.

7
Why Girls Choose Abusive Relationships

THE MOST FREQUENTLY asked questions I hear from parents are, Why has my daughter chosen an abusive boyfriend? And why does she remain in the relationship? I'm sure you've asked yourself the same questions. In this chapter I offer some explanations and try to give you a better understanding of your daughter's true goals in her teenage years—and the ways that she is not meeting those goals by remaining in an abusive relationship.

The most important task of your daughter's adolescence is to discover a sense of identity. This includes her search for her own beliefs and values and the type of person she would like to become. It is during this process that she examines the values you have instilled—including your sexual values—and decides if they are worthy of bringing into her adult life. While it may be uncomfortable to think of your daughter as a sexual being, with the hormones that are running rampant through her body at this stage it is basically a biological impossibility for her not to think about sex. It doesn't mean that you have done a poor job as a parent or that there is something fundamentally wrong with your daughter.

As parents, we hope that our children keep the values that we have instilled in them since they were very young. Although they may be rebellious at this stage in their lives, be assured that, in fact, your children will cling to the vast majority of your values and bring them into adulthood and into their own families.

Adolescents are primarily concerned with the way they appear to their peers. That is one reason girls are often desperate for a boyfriend in high school. If their friends are dating, they feel out of place if they are not. This may be one reason your daughter is willing to stay in her relationship, even though it is abusive and psychologically unhealthy.

Teens are asked very early in their high school careers to decide whether they are going on to higher education, and if so, what type: private college, state university, state college, community college, or vocational school. Their choice determines what type and level of classes they must attend in high school in order to meet college admission requirements. They are also asked to state their intended college major and, often, their choice of profession.

How can a fourteen- or fifteen-year-old know the answers to these questions? The pressure is on these kids not only to do well in their required classes but to take advanced-placement courses in order to achieve the highest possible grade-point average. In addition, they are told that college admissions officers look favorably upon involvement in school clubs and athletics, as well as outside community volunteer work. They must prepare for and excel at the SAT's. Many students avail themselves of an SAT-preparation course as well as a private college counselor. The competitive nature of the college system practically demands all of this pressure-filled activity in order to be considered for admission.

I attended UCLA in the mid-1970s, having had a B average in high school and ho-hum scores on my SAT's. My children would like to attend the same school and have been told not to bother filling out an application unless they have a 4.5 grade-point average and a minimum of 1,350 (out of 1,600) on the SAT's.

With all this unnatural pressure—college-level classes, a frenzy of extracurricular activities, and admissions-test preparation—when does your daughter have the time to attend to her real job of developing a sense of her own identity? The answer is that she doesn't. So she attaches herself to a boy who is cocky, sure of himself, charming, and seems to have all the answers. He tells her who she is, and because she hasn't investigated this process herself, she believes him. Of course, he is in the same boat as she is and only appears to know what he's doing.

She believes her boyfriend when he tells her she's nothing and no one else would want her. She thinks she had better stay with him because he's the best she's going to get, and it is unbearable to imagine being an outsider in a sea of boyfriends and girlfriends. By remaining in her abusive relationship, she hopes that she will be able to find herself.

If your daughter is not considering higher education or is not quite sure what she wants to do with her life, she may be even more susceptible to a relationship with an abusive boy. Without a particular career or path to follow, she's likely to count even more on her identity as "John's girlfriend."

Psychoanalyst Erik Erikson called this stage of adolescence "identity versus role confusion." He believed it is essential to develop a sense of identity in order to achieve the important task of intimacy in young adulthood. Erikson theorized that real intimacy was possible only once a sense of identity is developed. Only when the teenager is secure with her own identity is she able to lose herself in true mutuality with another person. Certainly, she feels that she is emotionally intimate with her boyfriend—and may confuse that with physical intimacy—but it is just an illusion. Sexual relations are not the same as intimacy. Erikson stated that when teens fail to attain genuine mutuality, they experience the opposite feeling: isolation. This is possibly the worst feeling a teenager can have, and girls in particular will do whatever is necessary in order to make sure that doesn't happen.

Why, then, did your daughter choose an abusive boyfriend? Many of the answers to this complex question will be answered in chapter 10, when we discuss family dynamics. Family dynamics are perhaps the most important indicator of whether a girl will choose an abusive boyfriend. For the purpose of our discussion here, however, there is a simple answer: he was not abusive at the beginning of the relationship. Then he was charming, complimentary, attentive, caring, and loving. Hearing "I love you" from a boy's mouth is a huge hook. Once he lands his catch—your daughter—he is free to act in whatever way serves him best. For the reasons stated earlier, it is very difficult for her to leave him.

During the teenage years, your daughter feels insecure about her appearance and behavior. If she has a pimple, she assumes that it looks like a huge flashing red light on her face, drawing the attention and horror of all those around her. If she gains a single pound, she might as well shop for clothes at Omar the Tentmaker. Extremes in feelings and behaviors are the norm. In addition, teenagers are notoriously narcissistic, believing that the sun rises and sets because of them. Put this combination together, and you can understand some of the reasons you and your daughter may not see eye-to-eye.

How many times have you said, "Why are you so sensitive?" "Why are you so illogical? You're not making any sense." "Why don't you listen to reason?" "Your face looks fine. I don't see any pimples." "Why do you stand in front of the mirror for half a day?" "You look fine in those pants. Stop making such a fuss."

Abusive boyfriends, who are the very definition of insecurity, take advantage of your daughter's insecurities about her appearance. While they initially pay her extensive and "heartfelt" compliments, these often turn into emotionally and verbally abusive behaviors, as stated in chapter 2. Because your daughter doesn't have an understanding of who she really is, she takes his hurtful comments very personally. But, she reasons, he tells me that he loves me, and who else would be interested in dating a blimp with zits? She's stuck and won't listen to your logic because you are her parents and "have" to say she's pretty, funny, and smart. Her boyfriend knows her better than you do. She is certain of that.

When I was sixteen, I felt like I was looking for something I lost. I didn't know what it was, but I just had that nagging feeling. It was sort of like the feeling you have when you go on vacation and you feel like you forgot to pack something. I was looking and looking but didn't know what I was looking for. It was really annoying.

I never had a boyfriend before I met Marc. I had guy friends but nobody who took me to dances and on real dates. I was pretty sure I'd never get one. Then Marc transferred to my school from out of town. He didn't seem like he ever felt out of place, even in a new high school, which is pretty intimidating. I wouldn't say he was Mr. Popularity, but he seemed sure of himself.

When my biology teacher assigned me the job of telling Marc what we had done so far that semester, I was glad. I wouldn't say he was the best-looking boy in the school, but he had this confidence that was very appealing.

We started eating lunch together and sort of hanging out after school. His favorite group was Nine Inch Nails. I'd heard their songs but didn't feel one way or another about them. I started really liking them through Marc. He had a good eye for color and clothing, which I didn't pay too much attention to. When he suggested that certain clothes would look good on me, I believed him. I didn't know where I wanted to go to college, so when he started talking to me about the schools he was interested in, I sent away for catalogs. I could go on and on, but it embarrasses me now to think about who I was, or wasn't, back then.

We broke up seven months later because he found another girl he was interested in more than me. I was sick about it, and seeing him in school every day was so hard. After I got over him, which took a pretty long time, I realized what I was looking so hard for before I met him: myself. —JENNA, NINETEEN

The next story illustrates what happens to a girl when she doesn't listen to her instincts about her abusive boyfriend. It also clearly demonstrates the tremendous pressure many girls encounter in trying to attract and keep a boyfriend at all costs.

Erica's Story

Sixteen-year-old Erica asked if she could speak with me after I had just given a presentation to her class. It was lunchtime, and she offered me half of the sandwich that was in her brown bag as we sat at the desks in her classroom.

Erica explained that she felt frightened now after hearing my lecture. She was afraid that her boyfriend might be an abuser, but she didn't know how to approach him or if she should leave the relationship. She began to cry.

She explained that her boyfriend was very controlling and told her how she should dress and how much makeup she should wear. Once when he decided that she had on too much lipstick he roughly wiped it off with the back of his hand, smearing it across her face. She said she felt "hurt and creepy" by that display but didn't say anything.

He phoned her frequently, often at odd hours of the night. One time her bedside telephone rang at two-thirty in the morning, startling her awake. There wasn't any answer on the other end of the phone, so she hung up. A moment later, she pressed *69, which calls the number of the person who phoned her last. His mother answered the phone. Erica apologetically explained that she thought her boyfriend had phoned her a moment earlier. His mother became angry and hung up. The next day Erica asked him why he had called her in the middle of the night. He looked stunned and then called her "nuts." Why would he call her at that hour? he asked. She now realized that he was checking up on her. Earlier that same day he had accused her of dating another boy at school. She explained that she didn't even know him, but he wouldn't listen to her.

Erica mentioned several other abusive behaviors, and it became clearer to her that her assumption about his being an abuser was correct. She cried again.

I asked Erica how many times she felt "creepy" about these behaviors. She told me she did every time. I asked her why she hadn't listened to her instincts and broken off the relationship earlier.

"Oh, Dr. Murray, you don't understand what it's like in high school now," she said through her tears. "You have to have a boyfriend, or everyone thinks there's something wrong with you. If you just hang out with girlfriends, rumors start circulating that you must be a lesbian. It's really horrible."

I was shocked. I knew about the pressure to have a boyfriend but didn't know that false accusations of sexual orientation were also a factor.

"It's not that easy to get a boyfriend if you break up with the one you have. In junior year almost everyone's taken. If you look like you're interested in just being friends with a guy, his girlfriend gets psycho and starts spreading rumors that you're a slut."

Erica told me a little about her academic record, and it was obvious that she was very intelligent and an extremely good student. Once again I was reminded that even smart girls get into abusive situations.

"It's really hard for me to get such good grades," she said. "I have to study a lot, and my boyfriend doesn't understand that. He never works at it and gets straight A's. He's just naturally brilliant. He resents that I study so much and is always interrupting me when I'm doing my homework. I'm under so much pressure to get good grades. My parents have worked so hard to save up for my college tuition, and they want me to go to a good school. They will have to take out loans to help pay for it. Good grades aren't enough to be accepted to these schools, so I also volunteer at the library and play volleyball. I'm so exhausted at the end of every day that I can barely do my homework. I sure don't have time to find another boyfriend."

Erica was in a difficult situation. She recognized that her boyfriend was abusive, but outside pressures made it impossible—in her mind—to change where she was. She didn't want to be the brunt of rumors, nor did she want to jeopardize the college career her parents had planned for her. All I could do was give her the facts so that she could predict what was probably coming down the pike for her if she stayed with her boyfriend. I asked her to consider whether her own self-worth and safety were worth the risks. I couldn't make the decision for Erica, but I hope she made a good choice.

8

Infatuation, Addictive Love, and Mature Love

AS PARENTS, we often make the mistake of feeling that our children are too young to fall in love or too inexperienced to understand what love is. This attitude discounts how they feel and is one more reason that our daughters can't come to us when they have a problem in a relationship. We've already told them that they're wrong or mistaken about their own feelings. When we tell them they can't trust what they are experiencing, we send a dangerous message, because your daughter's abuser also tells her how and what to think and feel.

When parents give their daughters messages that deny their feelings and sense of reality, it is for the parents' benefit and comfort, not the girl's. It gives the parents a false sense of security and control to believe that their daughter isn't old enough to experience romance. If their daughter stays young and childlike, she will not be hurt emotionally or sexually. Nonetheless, it is a fact of nature that our daughters are becoming women.

If, as parents, we can join our girls in the excitement of early love and *guide* them, they will have a more fulfilling experience and be more open to share it all, both the good and bad parts of the relationship. We need to communicate with our daughters so that they can stand up for themselves against predatory boyfriends.

It is my opinion that a fifteen-year-old understands as much about love as you do . . . for her age and level of experience. According to the Search Institute in Minneapolis, 39 percent of American fifth-graders said that they were currently in love.

Today's kids are exposed to romantic relationships far earlier than we were. However, throughout the ages, teen romance and the drama of being swept away by the passion and uncontrolled feelings that accompany it have endured. All we have to do is look at Shakespeare: *Romeo and Juliet* hasn't endured for hundreds of years without reason. It has a compelling theme: love at first sight, a couple of misunderstood teens, boy taking girl away from a stifling life, romantic sex shortly after they meet, and most important, tragedy and love being paired as one.

Even kids who wouldn't be caught dead reading the play were mesmerized by the most recent movie version starring Leonardo DiCaprio and Claire Danes in the title roles. It was the same story told in a modern way: star-crossed lovers having to meet in private because their parents don't understand them. Their love was so strong that eventually they sacrificed their lives to it. Wouldn't we be horrified if we learned that our fourteen-year-old daughter was involved with a boy in this way? The same theme runs through the television shows girls watch: *Dawson's Creek, Popular,* and the like. It's all over the radio as well, especially as sung by the new crop of female artists such as Alanis Morissette, Jewel, Sarah McLachlan, and Shawn Colvin. And let's not forget all of the romance novels geared toward teenage girls, the ones with junior Fabios on the cover.

Face it: girls are raised from the time they are toddlers to believe that love is magical, fantastical, and totally out of their control. If they are lucky, a wonderful prince will sweep them up, put a cheap plastic shoe on their foot, take them out of their dingy home where they are misunderstood and underappreciated, and gallop away with them into a wonderful future.

But wait a second: how much did Cinderella really know about Prince Charming? She knew he was a sharp dresser and a great dancer, and of course, he was drop-dead gorgeous. But did she know how he treated his mother? Did she know if he liked to smack women around because, after all, he was the prince and always held the power in the relationship? Of course he was charming—but so are most abusers! Maybe she should have gotten to know him better—but that wouldn't have been so romantic.

Why don't we give girls different role models for love? Well, as mothers we were raised on the same ideals. Maybe we believed we married a "prince" and then were disillusioned. Probably no one told us what we understand as we mature: a prince doesn't just appear in your life—you create a whole person in yourself and then seek out another whole person with whom to share your life. A woman or man cannot be half a person, hook up with another half a person, and create a whole relationship.

Some of the important messages we want to get across to our daughters are that love is not an out-of-control feeling—*love is a choice*. There isn't a thing called love at first sight, but there is lust at first sight. Sexual desire is not the same thing as love or caring behavior. Fairy tales are sweet, but they won't protect your daughter from abusers or prepare her for feelings she will have when she begins to date.

Let's take a few minutes now to talk about those feelings; the different types of love your daughter will experience; the signs you can look for at each stage of her relationship; and most important, the ways in which you can help her pass through these stages more successfully.

INFATUATION

Nearly all dating relationships, whether they are between adults or teens, begin with infatuation. There is a sense of excitement and romance, as well as a feeling of urgency. The partners can't wait to be together; they spend inordinate amounts of time talking on the phone, dreaming about each other, and seeing each other exclusively, often to the detriment of other friendships. Often, teens "know" they are in love because they have a queasy stomach, a headache, sweaty palms, and can't eat or sleep. If your daughter exhibits these symptoms, it's not mature love, it's infatuation—or the flu. The feeling is one of being carried away, and it is thrilling, much in the same way a roller-coaster ride is thrilling: it's dangerous, dizzying, and out of your control. If you've ever been on a roller-coaster, chances are you've either vomited and vowed never to do that again or thought it was so exciting you couldn't wait for another ride. Either way, it had an impact.

Infatuation is a great feeling and is a necessary part of love. It is the type of starry-eyed romance that all girls dream about. As you know, infatuation must always turn into mature love in order for a relationship to survive, although we hope to keep alive some of the passion, romance, and energy of this early stage.

We want to teach our daughters that during the infatuation stage, they ought to stand back and take a look at the boy's behaviors. Is she happy that he calls her several times each day to tell her that he loves her? She may later find that he is possessive and the frequent phone calls actually indicate that he needs to know where she is at all times. Is she flattered that he doesn't want her to talk with other guys? That not only shows insecurity on his part, but it may turn into unreasonable and stifling jealousy. Is it "so cute" the way he seems to forget little things? She may find later that he is selfish and doesn't ever forget anything that is important to him. You get the idea.

We also want to let our daughters know that they cannot carry on this *affaire de coeur* in secret. You have every right, as well as the responsibility, to meet and evaluate this young man by questioning him and chatting as parents do. Your child must know that it is not acceptable for her to go out with a boy you don't know anything about. After all, *your* eyes aren't glazed over with the newness of love. You have 20/20 vision.

We should also ask our daughters to look at their own behaviors in a new relationship. Does she feel anxious, jealous, out of control, overly accommodating? Does she forget about her other friends in order to spend every moment with him? Does she forsake her family, her own interests, or her schoolwork while waiting by the telephone for him to call? Why does she want to date only this one boy to the exclusion of finding out more about herself in dating others as well? Has he verbally and emotionally abused her by demeaning her appearance or told her that he's the only boy who would have her?

Let your daughter know that even while utterly infatuated, she is still in complete control of her behavior and responsible for her decisions regarding the relationship; if she is not, it gives a boy a perfect opportunity to feel that she wants to be dominated or doesn't really care how she is treated. Is that really what she wants to convey? Even though she is in love, she can still establish healthy boundaries for herself and the relationship.

Kathy started going out with Paul when she was fourteen. My wife and I thought it was a little young, but she convinced us that we were just old-fashioned and all kids that age were dating. We checked around, and several of the parents we spoke with said it was true. They were allowed to go to the movies together and things like that. We thought she was safe because we always drove them wherever they went. They talked on the phone all the time, and lots of those times she'd be crying. She was always saying she was sorry. My wife asked me, "What do you think a fourteen-year-old has to feel sorry about?" We tried talking to her, but she said she was just being stupid.

One day we heard her trying to defend herself with Paul over the phone, telling him that she loves only him and wouldn't ever even look at another boy again for as long as she lived because they were going to be together forever. We were so upset, I can't tell you. What was this forever stuff? My God, she was only fourteen. Of course she was going to look at other boys. We went into her room, I pushed my finger down on the receiver button, and I told her, "This conversation is over." She started sobbing. "You don't understand. I've upset him. It's all my fault. I'm afraid of what he's going to do to himself now. I didn't really like the other boy; I was just talking to him because he was in my class and we're working on a project together." This went on and on, with my wife and I thinking, "Who is this girl, and how did she take over our daughter's body?"

Over her protests, we called Paul's parents and told them what was going on and why Kathy wouldn't be dating him anymore. They laughed and thought we were being foolish, and that's just how kids talk. It seemed like whatever we did to trust our gut feelings, we were being told we were wrong and not in check with the times. My daughter was trying to bolt out of the house and actually hit my wife to get away from her. We were afraid she would run away in the middle of the night because she felt so responsible for Paul. She had exhausted herself with this frantic behavior, and we took turns staying with her all night. The next morning, we took her to a counseling center near us and started on a course of therapy for her and as a family. She had only known this boy for three weeks. —DEREK, FORTY-SEVEN

Fortunately, Kathy's story had a positive outcome. She and her parents entered into weekly family therapy, and I worked with Kathy individually as well. I am sure you can understand the desperation and fear Derek and his wife felt at the time. Their daughter was out of control and was unable to think clearly. Although this family's story is quite dramatic, it is not atypical of the situations parents tell me about. If your daughter's relationship has reached this serious stage, I encourage you to find immediate psychological assistance for your family. Legal steps may be necessary as well. Chapter 13 will outline your options in these areas.

Signs of Infatuation

- usually occurs at the beginning of a relationship
- physical and sexual attraction is central
- characterized by urgency, intensity, sexual desire, and anxiety
- driven by the excitement of being involved with a person whose character is not fully known
- involves nagging doubts and unanswered questions; the partner remains unexamined so as not to spoil the dream
- is based on fantasy
- is consuming, often exhausting
- entails discomfort with individual differences
- relationship not enduring because it lacks a firm foundation

When I first started going out with Vince, it was like heaven on earth. I felt so great around him and loved every minute we were together. He was very strong and dynamic. He knew exactly what he wanted to do, and it made me feel great about myself just being around him. I liked that he had lots of friends, because I was so shy and thought that going with him would make me come out of my shell.

Actually it didn't, and I just became jealous of the time he spent with his friends, especially girls who he knew as pals long before he knew me. If I wasn't with him, I worried about what he was doing and questioned his love for me all the time. We spent a lot of time on the phone, usually two or three hours each night, after we saw each other during and after school. I thought about him constantly and wanted to be with him all the time. All this happened just in the first couple of months we were dating.

I don't know exactly what happened to us; I think we kind of wore each other out. We just sort of fizzled, but not because of a fight or anything. He just started calling less and less, and I guess I got involved in other things. I do remember that I was always

*tired when we were dating, and afterward, although I was really
sad, I also had more energy and started doing things I liked to do
again.* —MARIE, SEVENTEEN

Marie experienced a healthy ending to her infatuation with
Vince. It is important to know that infatuation will always fizzle out
at some point. If the relationship doesn't end, it then becomes
either addictive or mature love.

ADDICTIVE LOVE

If you are reading this book because you are concerned that your
daughter is in a dangerous relationship, she probably feels addictive love for her boyfriend. Perhaps you've tried to talk with her and
given her every good reason why she shouldn't be with him. If she
is involved in addictive love, she cannot listen to logic.

Let's think about addicts for a moment. Perhaps at one time you
or someone you know was addicted to cigarettes, alcohol, or drugs.
It is not possible to tell that person, "You know, using this substance is really bad for you. It could kill you. You should stop using
it right now and never think about it again." Although your daughter is not chemically addicted to this boy, she has an emotional
compulsion to be with him that is every bit as strong as a drug.

If your daughter is in this type of relationship, she believes that
she can't live without him and feels desperate when they aren't together. She is terrified of being alone. Because of this feeling, she
may engage in activities that she wouldn't normally engage in, such
as substance abuse, being verbally or physically abusive to her family, sex, lying, and cheating. Students in addictive relationships become C or D students. You may see your daughter's future going up
in flames.

Many parents tell me that they don't even recognize their daughter since she started dating the current creep, that this isn't the girl
they raised: "We used to have such a close relationship. She was a
good student and was involved in school activities. She liked to go

out with her girlfriends and always told us where she was going. We didn't worry about her a bit. Then she got messed up with him and became a different person."

Sound familiar? Your daughter is addicted to a boy. Just in the same way that addicts will do anything for a fix, your daughter is willing to risk everything to stay with him.

Being in an addictive relationship puts your daughter at greater risk of being sexually and physically abused because the boy can easily take advantage of her addictive state. He knows that she will do anything for him because she's desperate. More important, he knows that she will take anything from him as long as she gets her fix. This gives him permission to treat her any way he likes, knowing that her greatest fear is withdrawal of "affection."

> *I have to admit now that I was abusive to my former girlfriend. I used to dog her all the time. I'd go out with other girls and tell her about it just to see her reaction. I'd tell her she was stupid in algebra or try to jinx her exams right before she took them. I did all this stuff because I could. I mean, she let me.*
>
> *Luckily for her, her parents put their foot down and made her end the relationship. Our school counselor saw how she was upset all the time and was talking to her. After we broke up, she called me into her office and told me that all the stuff I was doing to her was because I was insecure and scared to lose her. She said that my girlfriend wasn't the weaker one in the relationship—I was, because a real man doesn't have to treat a woman like that in order to keep her. It kind of spun my head around.*
>
> —ANTHONY, SIXTEEN

How many times have you seen your daughter cry this week? How many times has she apologized to the boy for things she didn't even do just to stop an argument? Has she stopped making plans with her girlfriends or her family, just in case he calls or wants to see her? Do you feel that she has become more distant from you? Does she appear to understand that this relationship is destructive and promises to break it off, only to go back with him time after time? She's addicted.

Much of this book is devoted to helping you talk with your daughter about this relationship in a way that she will be able to hear, as well as offering steps to free her from this boy. Please understand that in this case, as with all addicts, until she is ready to take the steps, some of the solution is out of your control. Helplessness is the worst feeling a parent can have.

Krystal was always a happy and popular girl. Everyone seemed to love her. She's not a genius, but she always worked hard at school and got mostly B's. She and I were both so excited when she made the swim team and was the fourth swimmer on the relay team because she was so strong. She brought home medals from her swim meets and put them on her wall.

She went out with a couple of young men she had met through swimming, and they seemed very nice. Things were going great for Krystal, and we even thought that she might be eligible for a college scholarship for swimming. I've been a single parent since she was three, and her father hardly ever sent support checks, so I've had to work hard to support us. I was proud that she was going to have more opportunities than I did, since I became pregnant with her at eighteen.

Then she met Joe, and almost overnight her whole life changed. He dropped out of high school but sometimes hung around the campus, visiting friends of his. He met Krystal one day when she was fumbling for change in her purse to buy a Coke. He offered to buy it for her. She came home and told me what an old-fashioned gentleman he was, and I thought, "Oh, that's sweet, another nice boy." He was nice just long enough to rope her in and get her hooked, which I'm embarrassed to say took only two weeks.

She waited by the phone for his calls. She spent so much time with him that she didn't have time to study. Her teachers called me in for conferences because they saw such a rapid decline. She didn't do things with her friends and chased away any other boys who called. She stopped going to swim practice because he thought she was showing off her body in her swimsuit. She was eventually kicked off the team.

One time I heard them arguing in the living room. I came in to see him pinning her against the wall with one hand and the other hand punched in the wall next to her face. I called the police. By the time they got here, he had gone, but of course Krystal was terrified and so was I. But what she was afraid of wasn't the violence—it was of losing him! I couldn't believe what I was hearing.

The police suggested that I get a restraining order, which I did. Krystal didn't want to enforce it, but I enlisted neighbors who were home when I wasn't to call the police if they saw him at the house. I also told the school, and they called the police when he came onto the campus. He was released to his parents' custody three times, and then they brought him to juvenile detention.

It took Krystal a long time to get over him, and I don't want to think about what her life would be like today if he wasn't sent away. I doubt that she would even be alive. —MARCY, THIRTY-SIX

Signs of an Addictive Relationship

- a feeling of not being able to live without the partner
- insecurity, distrust, lack of confidence, feeling threatened
- low self-esteem; looking to partner for validation and affirmation of self-worth
- fewer happy times together; more time spent on apologies, fear, guilt, and unkept promises
- needing the other in order to feel complete
- feeling worse about oneself as the relationship progresses
- loss of self-control
- making fewer decisions or plans; waiting for the partner to tell what to do
- discomfort with individual differences

- tearing down or criticizing the other
- feeling as though one is "killing time" until with partner again
- rushing things, like sex or marriage, so as not to lose the partner
- breaking promises to oneself or others because of the relationship
- being threatened by the other partner's growth
- constant jealousy and insecurity
- using drugs or alcohol as coping mechanisms
- friends or family report that the person is "different" from the way she used to be

When Rob and I first met, it was great. We were together all the time because we felt like we just clicked, you know? We felt like we had found our true soul mate. Of course, we had only known each other for three days when we felt that way. We got very involved really quickly, if you know what I mean. Anyway, I lost my virginity to him less than a week after we met because we had already talked about being together forever.

We spent every moment together. If we weren't together in person, we were on the phone or writing love notes to each other—well, actually more me to him. I stopped going places with my friends and even turned down a great class trip to Mexico because I didn't want to be away from him for five days. After a couple of weeks, my friends became pretty disgusted with me, but I didn't really care. He started seeing his friends again, and that always upset me because he wasn't with me. I'd wait by the phone for him to call me. Sometimes he wouldn't get home until really late, and I didn't do my homework all night because I was waiting for him to call and that was the only thing on my mind. I grew so dependent on him and was so afraid of not being with him. After a couple of months, all I had in my life was him. He eventually broke up with me, but I still don't trust myself to know what a good relationship should be like. —RENEE, SIXTEEN

In both Marcy's and Renee's sad stories, the girls were addicts. They were constantly on edge and felt desperate. They gave up almost everything in their lives in order to be with boyfriends who treated them badly.

MATURE LOVE

Unfortunately for teenagers, mature love is depicted on film and in print as old-fogey love. It's boring and predictable, not exciting, passionate, or adventurous like infatuation. It's what you settle for when you give up on your youth and dreams and are happy with a nine-to-five job, the ol' ball and chain, and a frozen dinner served on a TV tray in front of Dan Rather. There's none of the drama and angst teens crave.

Of course, what teenagers don't realize is that infatuation can only last so long, and if a relationship is to survive and prosper, it must move on to mature love. The two main characteristics of mature love are that it is energizing in a healthy way and that it is based on reality.

In a mature love relationship, you want at least as much for your partner as you do for yourself, and you encourage your partner's growth. Unlike infatuation or addictive love, mature love doesn't involve jealousy, for each partner is secure in his or her partner's affection. Unlike infatuation, in a mature relationship each partner encourages the other to enjoy friends and activities both individually and together.

Girls in mature relationships don't feel they must be perfect or overly accommodating in order to keep their boyfriend's attention. Nor do they feel that they can't express disappointment or an honest opinion. In a mature love relationship, both partners find that they like each other even more the longer they are together and the more they know about each other. However, they don't make excuses for poor behavior or deny that difficulties exist. In time, they learn to solve problems together and don't feel as if they will break up every time they have a spat.

As parents, you should be thrilled that your daughter has reached this stage, right? Well, yes and no. It's comforting to see your daughter slow down from the infatuation stage and go back to a more normal routine. But it comes with its own challenges. This is a good time to have another talk with your daughter—and her boyfriend, if you feel comfortable—about your rules regarding sex. During this stage your daughter feels safe, settled, and that her relationship might last a long time. Often teens feel that they've been together long enough to make a decision about sex. Although this type of talk may be uncomfortable for you, it is necessary for your daughter's safety. She and her boyfriend should know in the greatest detail possible what you expect of them regarding sex.

If you say, "No sex allowed," does that mean intercourse only, or does it include oral and manual sex? Does it mean that touching each other over their clothes is permissible? If you feel that no matter what you say, they will probably have sex anyway, will you offer to take your daughter to your gynecologist for an examination, education, and birth control? Will you talk with both kids about safer sex and exactly how to use a condom? Do your daughter and her boyfriend understand your rules about permissible conduct in your home? I feel you squirming in your chair right now; however, if you aren't candid with your daughter about this subject, you are not only being naïve, you are possibly putting her in a more difficult situation later.

Some parents who decide that safe sex is permissible take the policy that they would rather their daughter have sex in their home than in a car or alley. This may sound ludicrous to you, but it is something to consider at this stage of her relationship. Is her boyfriend allowed in her bedroom while you're at home? Are doors to remain open? Is her curfew later if they stay home than if they go out?

It's also important to check in with your daughter frequently. Is her schoolwork up to its usual level? Is she enjoying other friends and activities apart from her boyfriend? Since you also want to let the boy know that you are a constant presence in your daughter's life, be sure to invite him to the house often for dinner, family gatherings, pool parties, and so on. They won't feel the need to be sneaky if you are a part of their relationship.

> *At first I was worried that I would miss the drama and excitement of my early relationship with Tim. But to tell you the truth, it was so tiring in those days. I was running here and there with him, taking two or three showers a day, always making sure I was wearing makeup, holding in my stomach, and worrying if my breath wasn't fresh. I must have single-handedly supported the Certs company.*
>
> *I thought that if we stayed together, I'd have to settle for a boring relationship like I thought my parents had. I guess in some ways it got sort of predictable, but in a nice kind of way. We were together for two years, and then he was accepted to a college back east. I considered going with him, but I knew that I didn't want to be away from my parents, grandparents, and girlfriends.*
>
> *It was really hard to see him go and know that realistically we wouldn't be able to keep our relationship long distance and we'd both find other people. But we cared about each other so much that we both wanted the other to feel happy and content, which meant that we should have the option of going out with people nearby. We've stayed in touch and are probably each other's closest friend still, but we aren't going together as boyfriend and girlfriend anymore. We both have other people in our lives.*
>
> —FRANNIE, NINETEEN

Signs of Mature Love

- develops gradually through learning about each other
- sexual attraction is present, but warm affection/friendship is central
- characterized by calm, peacefulness, empathy, support, trust, confidence, and tolerance of each other; no feelings of being threatened

- driven by deep attachment; based on extensive knowledge of both positive and negative qualities in the other person; mature acceptance of imperfections
- partners want to be together but are not obsessed with the relationship
- is based on reality
- is energizing in a healthy way
- partners have high self-esteem; each has a sense of self-worth with or without the partner and feels complete even without the relationship
- individuality is accepted
- each brings out the best in the other; relationship is nurturing
- partners are patient, feel no need to rush the events of the relationship; there is a sense of security and no fear of losing the partner
- each encourages the other's growth
- is enduring and sustaining because it is based on a strong foundation of friendship

WHAT YOU CAN DO NOW

This is a good opportunity to go over the signs of each type of relationship with your daughter and ask her to realistically check off the characteristics in each column that she honestly feels apply to her relationship. You can do the same and then compare notes. Remember—if you check off everything in the addictive category and none of the characteristics of mature love, you may not be opening the dialogue you would like. If she feels that you understand her boyfriend is not 100 percent monster and you appreciate the one good quality he does have, she is more likely to listen to you. In this way, you can focus on the ways in which she is acting healthfully and taking care of herself in this relationship.

It may take some effort to do this, since you think this guy is slime. For instance, you can say something like, "I really respect that you and Bob feel that you're going to get married someday but have made a decision to finish high school first. That's so important for your future and shows me that you can make good decisions in this area." This not only supports her, it also gives her the subtle message that you expect her to graduate.

This is a time to open communication, not to interrogate. Let her know that you understand the way it feels to be so in love. You may want to tell a few stories of your own teenage romances—both good and bad relationships. Our children often believe that dinosaurs roamed the earth when we were their age. This is a great opportunity to be real with your daughter, instead of an old person who couldn't possibly understand the way she feels.

In a soothing manner, you can rationally explain to your daughter your concerns for her health—emotionally and physically—as well as her safety. If possible, try your best not to criticize her boyfriend. Remember, you do not have the power to change her boyfriend's behavior. Your hope at this stage is to influence your daughter's thinking about her place in the relationship. Ultimately, the responsibility is hers, not his. When we believe that our happiness is based on another person's feelings or behaviors, that is codependent thinking: I'm okay if you're okay. It is also living reactively rather than actively.

In my work as a therapist, talking with thousands of high school students each year, I have found that many teenage girls live by reacting to their boyfriend's moods and wishes. Virtually all girls in abusive relationships do this. Now is the time to point this behavior out to her and invite her to study her own thoughts and desires.

There are many more steps you can take; they are outlined in chapter 13.

Above all, remember that you are your daughter's safe place to fall. Let her know that she has your support, so that she understands that she can always go home.

9 The Role of Alcohol and Drugs

THE USE OF ALCOHOL and drugs has risen astronomically since you were a teenager. Before we begin discussing the ways in which an abusive boyfriend who is also abusing substances can damage your daughter, let me share some "sobering" statistics with you.

- According to the National Council on Alcoholism, alcohol is the most widely used and abused drug in America. In fact, one tenth of the drinking population consumes one half of the alcoholic beverages sold.
- There are more than ten million alcoholics in the United States.
- Alcohol is involved in 60 percent of reported cases of child abuse, a majority of domestic-violence cases, 41 percent of assaults, 39 percent of rapes, and 64 percent of criminal homicides.
- Thirty-five to 64 percent of drivers in fatal car accidents have been drinking. Of pedestrians killed, 25 percent have been drinking.

- Eighty percent of suicide victims were drinking before they took their lives.
- Children of alcoholics have a four times greater risk of developing alcoholism than children of nonalcoholics. There are 28.6 million children of alcoholics in the United States.
- An estimated 3.3 million drinking teenagers aged fourteen to seventeen are showing signs that they may develop serious alcohol-related problems.
- Recent surveys conducted in the United States indicate that the first drinking experience today usually occurs around age twelve. It is no longer unusual for ten- to twelve-year-olds to have serious alcohol-abuse problems.
- Since 1966 the number of high school students nationwide who are intoxicated at least once a month has more than doubled, from 10 percent to 20 percent. Alcohol-recovery experts estimate that that figure is grossly understated.
- Young Caucasian males drink more than any other group in the United States.
- According to Donald Goodwin, author of *Alcoholism: The Facts,* the eighteen-to-twenty-four age group has the highest proportion of heavy drinkers, with a marked rise in teenage drunkenness in the last few years.
- Most youths begin to drink in adolescence. A recent study on adolescent alcohol abuse found that alcohol is the most widely used drug by youths ages twelve to seventeen.
- About 30 percent of fourth-grade respondents to a *Weekly Reader* poll reported peer pressure to drink.
- Of 27,000 New York public-school students in grades seven through twelve, 11 percent described themselves as being hooked on alcohol.
- High school seniors responding to a national survey reported that nine out of ten had tried alcohol by age seventeen.
- Alcohol-related highway deaths are the number-one killer of fifteen-to-twenty-four-year-olds.

It is an undeniable fact that teens are using alcohol at a higher level than could previously be imagined. It is another unfortunate fact that alcohol and drug use are present in the great majority of abusive teen relationships. What does that mean for your daughter? If her boyfriend drinks or uses drugs—even recreationally—she is placing herself at great risk.

> *When Steve drank, he turned into a different person. He acted like he didn't care about what he said to me or how he treated me. It really hurt my feelings. A lot of the time he'd make me cry and tell me to shut up. Sometimes he'd grab me if I was trying to walk away from him. When he was sober, he'd tell me he was sorry and it wasn't him that was talking; it was the booze. After he did this for about six months, I finally asked him, "If you know that drinking makes you treat me bad, why do you keep drinking?" His only answer was "Because I like it." What I finally realized was that what he liked was that he had this alibi to do what he really wanted to do when he was sober.* —KATE, SEVENTEEN

Alcohol is accessible to most teens; most parents keep some in the home, and it is easily purchased, even by thirteen-year-olds. Drugs are just as readily available.

There are certain drugs that are most popular with teens at this time: marijuana, crack cocaine, crystal meth, Ecstasy, ketamine, Rohypnol, and chemical solvents (bear in mind that, like clothing, the popularity of specific drugs changes quite often).

Listed in the box on page 105 are the drugs most commonly used by teens, as well as signs to look for in your daughter and/or her boyfriend.

Ketamine—also known as "Special K"—is a popular nightclub drug. It is actually an animal tranquilizer. The difference between a recreational dose of ketamine and an overdose is dangerously small.

"Roofie" (Rohypnol) and GHB (also known as "Easy Lay") are both easily slipped into a soda. These drugs make a girl feel very

DRUG	PHYSICAL SIGNS	BEHAVIORAL SYMPTOMS
Alcohol	Clumsiness, staggering, slurred speech, odor of alcohol	Confusion, lack of concentration, mood changes quickly to depression or violence, nausea and vomiting
Cocaine/ crack/ Ecstasy	Inability to sit still, difficulty sleeping, fast breathing, dilated pupils, little or no appetite	Violent behavior, paranoia, hallucinations, increased desire for sex
Marijuana	Redness in eyes, sleepiness, dry mouth and lips, blurred vision	Slowed reaction time, altered sense of time, memory loss, paranoia
Crystal meth	Nasal bleeding, dry skin and sores, sweating, blurred vision, twitching and jerking in the face and extremities, severe weight loss	Aggression and hostility, paranoia, panic, restlessness, unusual talkativeness, anxiety and nervousness, moodiness, false self-confidence, extreme depression, hallucinations, bizarre compulsions
Inhalants	Slurred speech, sneezing, coughing, bloody nose, urinating and defecating without control, blue cast to skin	Dizziness, severe headaches, nausea, tiredness
PCP	Blurred eyesight, slurred speech, slower body movements	Hallucinations, increased strength, extreme paranoia, memory loss
ketamine ("Special K"), Rohypnol ("Roofie"), GHB ("Easy Lay")	Clumsiness, staggering, slurred speech	Confusion, lack of concentration

drunk and uncoordinated, thereby making her easy prey to date rape. Both drugs can be fatal.

Ecstasy (MDMA) is very popular among high school students. Studies have shown definitive and irreversible brain damage in monkeys and rodents that are administered this drug.

Thinking about these behaviors and symptoms, you can once again relate drug use to abusive behaviors, especially in terms of anxiety, irritability, and paranoia. Although there is a hot debate over legalizing the recreational use of marijuana, it cannot be overstated that, in most instances, pot is a gateway drug to harder substances. To be precise, while it cannot be said that all marijuana users will definitely go on to use crack or heroin, it can be stated that, almost without exception, all hard drug users began their experimentation with marijuana.

One of the problems with pot smoking in teens is that chronic use interferes with the endocrine system. That means that physical, emotional, and mental development may be impeded for eleven to fifteen years. Another difficulty—and one that is most critical for you and your daughter—is that many users experience anxiety, fear, and paranoia. Can you see the ways in which these psychological aspects play into abusive behavior? The effects of smoking pot can last for two days in the brain. In addition, the brain doesn't finish developing until a child is approximately twenty years old. One of the last regions to develop in the brain is the one involved with the ability to plan and make complex decisions.

I could go on about the reasons one becomes a substance abuser, but the only important one as it relates to your daughter is that substance abusers use drugs and alcohol to escape problems. These problems may be familial, school-related, or social. If your daughter is a rescuer, she may "understand" that he uses drugs in response to his difficult situation. It is important for her to know the following:

His substance use is voluntary. Every time he takes a drink, lights up, pops a pill, or snorts, he is making a conscious decision to get high. He is therefore deciding to escape his problems rather than deal with them in a mature manner.

> *I really don't want to deal with anything in my life right now. My parents are getting a divorce, and they've put me in the middle of it. I hate school. My friends have become idiots. I asked a girl that I like out, and she turned me down. All I want to do is get high.*
>
> —RYAN, SEVENTEEN

When her boyfriend is high, he cannot be expected to make rational or reasonable decisions. This is true not only for himself but for her as well. Some girls excuse their boyfriend's abusive behavior by stating, "He didn't mean it. He was just drunk and didn't know what he was saying." Perhaps he didn't. However, he made a decision to use and therefore not be responsible for his abusive behavior.

Rage and paranoia are increased when drugs are involved. This "allows" abusive behavior to become more extreme and feeds the boy's insecurity and dependence. If he is using, it is not possible for your daughter to tell her boyfriend that she wasn't looking at another boy, wasn't having sex with another boy, is not trying to make him jealous, and the like. He is high and is therefore more paranoid and enraged.

> *Rick is always accusing me of cheating on him when he's drunk. He takes me to parties and gets wasted, then tells me I'm fooling around with his friends. He's crazy when he drinks.*
>
> —BRITTANY, FIFTEEN

The opportunity for physical abuse increases in a drug-using boyfriend because of the inherent propensity to act out ragefully. While her boyfriend may "just" be verbally or emotionally abusive while sober, she is taking great risks with her safety when he is using. As stated earlier, this type of behavior ultimately presents itself even when the boy is not under the influence.

Len is like a Jekyll and Hyde character. When he's not stoned, he's pretty nice to me, although we do get in arguments. When he's doing [crystal] meth, he gets very physical. He pushes me around and pulls my hair. I'm afraid of him when he's using, but I'm too afraid of him to say anything. I mean, if he could be that way when I don't do anything to get him mad, I don't know what would happen if I said that when he was wasted. —LIZ, SIXTEEN

Drinking and drugs do not cause violence, but they allow your daughter's boyfriend to loosen his inhibitions and become violent. At that time both he and your daughter may use the excuse that the alcohol caused his violence, but as previously stated, *first* he made the decision to use.

Another dynamic to consider is that your daughter may be using alcohol or drugs to "keep him company." She may feel that this is a good way to show that she cares about him. This is treacherous and is more common than you may realize. When a girl uses with her boyfriend for these reasons, she is implying, "I care more about keeping my sick relationship going than about my own safety and health."

You have undoubtedly heard the term *codependent*. What I have just described is codependent behavior. The following is a checklist of characteristics of codependency as described by Melody Beattie in her book *Codependent No More*. Show them to your daughter, and ask her to check off the behaviors she sees in herself.

Codependents

1. ignore problems or pretend they aren't happening
2. pretend circumstances aren't as bad as they are
3. tell themselves things will be better tomorrow
4. stay busy so they don't have to think about things
5. get depressed or sick
6. become workaholics (overachieve in school or sports)
7. spend money compulsively

8. overeat
9. watch problems get worse
10. believe lies
11. lie to themselves
12. wonder why they feel like they're going crazy

Your daughter may be using drugs or alcohol as a self-medicating coping mechanism. Just as her boyfriend abuses substances to temporarily forget his problems, she may be doing the same thing relative to her relationship. She may be so miserable with him—and feel there is no way out—that she actually uses drugs rather than confront the problem.

> *I didn't want to think about giving up my boyfriend. It made me too afraid to even imagine it. I was crying all the time because I was so unhappy, but the thought of starting all over again made me sick. The only time I had some peace was when I was high. I didn't have to think about what a mess my life had become.*
>
> —DEBBY, SIXTEEN

If you suspect that your daughter is using drugs or alcohol, this is one of the times that I feel you are not only justified but obligated to invade her privacy and obtain information and proof by any means possible. Are you going to allow your daughter's health, safety, and possibly her life to be jeopardized because she has a boyfriend who uses drugs, encouraging her to do the same? Likewise, I'm sure you wouldn't allow her to use drugs to escape the fact that she is in an abusive relationship.

Please read this next point carefully. If your daughter is drinking or using drugs, she becomes an easy target for her boyfriend's abusive behaviors. As I mentioned earlier, he doesn't have good judgment when he is high. She doesn't either, under the same circumstances. She doesn't know that she can remove herself from a violent situation, and she has lost the ability to act in her own interest.

Help your daughter to understand that, aside from everything else she is jeopardizing, by using drugs she is also putting herself at great risk to be at the receiving end of her boyfriend's abuse. I'm sure you will offer her professional assistance in getting and staying off drugs. If she refuses your help, you will be able to see very clearly that your daughter has made a conscious decision to stay in her relationship and be an active participant in the abuse at this time. Do keep in mind, however, that if your daughter is a minor, you have the right to place her in a drug-treatment facility without her consent. It may be the most loving favor you ever do for her.

> *My friends used to tell me that I acted stupid at parties when I drank a lot. I was mean, and I know I had sex with guys I didn't care anything about. I put myself in a lot of risk, and thank God I didn't get hurt or pregnant or worse. My friends finally showed me a video that one of them took at a party, and I was disgusted with myself. I quit cold turkey and haven't touched liquor since. I know I have an addictive personality and wouldn't be able to manage having just one beer.* —BECKY, SEVENTEEN

As I mentioned in chapter 6, we now know that the age at which a person begins seriously using drugs or alcohol is the age at which he or she remains *emotionally* unless he gets real help with his addiction. (The word *seriously* is used broadly here, since one person's level of drug dependence may be different from another's. For our purposes, I will define *serious* as regular or frequent use.) This brings up a critical question to ask your daughter if her boyfriend is a user. Let's say he started smoking pot at age thirteen and by age fourteen was mixing it with alcohol. Let's even say that he never progressed to harder drugs but smokes almost daily and gets extremely drunk on the weekends.

Ask your daughter, "Considering that there is scientific proof that a person remains emotionally at the same stage as when they started using drugs or alcohol, when you are twenty-five, would you ever consider marrying a thirteen-year-old boy? Would you think that a thirteen-year-old boy would make a good father to your children? What kind of provider would a thirteen-year-old make for your family? Do you think that a thirteen-year-old boy could be on the same level of maturity as you would be when you are twenty-five? What kind of problems would you anticipate in that kind of relationship?"

The purpose of these questions is to help your daughter analyze the reality of her situation in the face of proof, as researched by the medical community, not just as your opinion. In addition, the questions aid her in thinking about what *she would like* for her future, not only in the present. It also helps her to shake herself of illogical, romantic *feeling* and get back to logical *thinking*.

That concept is the essence of a very effective and widely used form of therapy known as cognitive behavioral therapy. The bottom line is that dysfunction is based on irrational and faulty beliefs. The therapist's job is to help the client confront those beliefs and test the evidence for them; in doing so, the client will have to change her belief system to a healthier way of thinking. I ask clients to pretend that I am a judge in a courtroom and they are an attorney pleading a case. The client must logically convince me that the facts, not feelings, of their relationship are both healthy and productive. Similarly, you want to confront your daughter's faulty beliefs, those that are not founded in factual evidence, at every turn. This approach will not only help her in surviving the situation she now faces with an abusive boyfriend, it will aid her in problem-solving throughout her life.

> *My boyfriend used to do stupid things that only a kid would do. He would throw tantrums over the dumbest stuff that didn't even matter, and he'd insist on getting his way all the time. If he did something wrong, he'd say, "You won't tell my parents, will you?" He was into doing crack with his friends, which I hated. Every time I asked him to stop, he'd say, "I'm going to smoke as much as I want, and you can't make me stop."* —DEDE, SEVENTEEN

Felicia's Story

Felicia was a young woman who lived at the domestic-violence shelter where I worked. She was barely twenty years old, with a two-year-old son, and was five months pregnant by someone other than her son's father. Looking at Felicia, one could easily see that she was once a beautiful girl. Now, however, her strawberry blond hair was unkempt and brittle and her blue eyes looked dead and discouraged. Her skin was sallow, and she generally looked beaten down by life and her own abusive behaviors.

Felicia was proud that she had been clean and sober for seven months, but she had used drugs extensively for five years before that. She suspected that her son had developmental delays due to her drug use during pregnancy, and she worried that the baby she was carrying would be affected as well, even though she had stopped using drugs two months before the baby's conception. She wisely understood that the effects of drug use remain in the body long after the user has stopped.

Felicia didn't remember whether she began her drug use to self-medicate while in an abusive dating relationship or if she began using drugs and so attracted an abusive boyfriend. She only knew that the two things happened in quick succession.

Felicia started using drugs when she was fifteen. A friend offered her marijuana at a party. Her parents were very strict, and drug use had never entered her mind. But she didn't want to feel out of place at the party, so she tried a few puffs. To her surprise, she enjoyed it, and ended up smoking three joints that night. That quickly led to frequent use of the substance with new drug-using friends and with a boy to whom she lost her virginity while they were both stoned.

On her sixteenth birthday one of her friends introduced her to cocaine, and she became addicted fairly quickly. She loved how she felt while using it: confident, unafraid, outgoing, and fun to be around. While she originally snorted cocaine only at parties, she rapidly advanced to using it every weekend, then several times a week. Her parents were unaware of the signs of substance use and never suspected that their child had even tried drugs.

Felicia didn't have the money to buy cocaine, so she began exchanging sex for drugs. It didn't matter to her who the man was, as long as he'd supply her with the coke.

When she found out she was pregnant, she had already run away from home and was living beneath a freeway overpass in downtown Los Angeles. She didn't discover the pregnancy until she was almost seven months along. Since she was almost always "coked up," she didn't pay attention to her lack of menstruation and was used to feeling nauseous, tired, and weak while she was coming off the drug. The baby was fairly quiet and didn't kick much. It wasn't until a fellow drug user told her she was getting fat that she took a good look at her stomach and realized she must be pregnant. She never went to a doctor for fear that her drug use would be discovered and her parents would take her home to Spokane.

During her pregnancy, she was being beaten regularly by her dope supplier and anyone else who cared to do so. Although it bothered her, Felicia never said anything because she was afraid she would be cut off from her drugs. She knew she had bruises over much of her body and had been hit in the stomach more than once.

Felicia gave birth to her son in a park at night. A friend who was with her helped deliver the child. She didn't remember all the details but was told later that a passerby called the paramedics, who took her and the baby to the hospital.

While she was in the hospital, her baby was taken away to a safe place and was eventually placed with a foster family. She stayed in the hospital for three days and was released with the advice to get off the drugs. She suffered terrible withdrawal symptoms in the hospital.

She tried to see her baby but was told that Children's Protective Services were in charge of the case and the baby had his own advocate. She was forbidden to see her child while she was still an active drug user. If she wanted to have any future contact with him, she would have to admit herself into a drug treatment program. She did so, and after she tested clean for six months, her baby was released to her.

It didn't take long before the stress of caring for a baby drove her to the most familiar way she could think of to ease bad feelings. She found another drug supplier and began using cocaine once again.

During a home visit, her social worker saw many signs of Felicia's drug use: the apartment was filthy and the baby was dirty. His diaper hadn't been changed in so long that he had welts on his buttocks and penis. She took the baby away once again.

This time, Felicia was told that she was a danger to the baby and would have to discontinue her drug use for good if she was ever to see her child again. They told her they were only going to give her one more chance and then they would close the case for good.

Her parents flew to Los Angeles to admit her into an inpatient drug rehabilitation program, rented an apartment for themselves, and encouraged Felicia's sobriety. She was eventually released and did not go back to drugs; however, her pattern of abusive relationships with men had not been broken.

She had a series of torturous affairs, one of which resulted in her current pregnancy. She not only feared for her life, she also now knew that her son, with whom she had only recently been reunited, would be taken from her forever if he were in an abusive home. She also recognized that she didn't want to bring a new child into the world in that environment.

Felicia stayed in the shelter where I worked for the requisite six weeks, during which she received prenatal care and extensive therapy for herself and about the difficult relationship she had with her son, who was already quite aggressive toward her.

Felicia decided to go back to Spokane and live with her parents, where her baby was born. She is still in recovery from her past drug use and continues to attend Twelve-Step meetings and parenting courses.

How to Prevent Abuse in the First Place

Family Dynamics

THIS MAY BE the most difficult chapter in this book for you to read. I want you to know up front that I appreciate that, and my intention is not to blame, judge, criticize, or call you a bad guy. By addressing the elements of parental responsibility that "helped" your daughter get into her abusive relationship with her boyfriend, we can begin to see a way to help her get out.

Girls do not choose abusive relationships by accident; nor do they become the targets of abusive boyfriends without reason. If you take a good and honest look at your own family, you will see some of the ways in which the arrival of your daughter's boyfriend could have been predicted.

As parents, we are the most important role models our children will ever have. They incorporate our values and beliefs and learn from us what constitutes acceptable behavior, both in childhood and adult life. Children watch our actions more than they listen to our words. It is most important, therefore, that the behaviors we show them are consistent not only with our belief system but also with what we wish for them to emulate.

ABUSIVE HOMES

In chapter 6 I stated that one of the strongest indicators that a boy will become abusive is having been raised in an abusive home. That includes both being abused himself and watching his mother or sister being abused by his father. Likewise, one of the biggest indicators that a girl will become the recipient of abuse is a history of abuse in her family. Why is this so? When a girl observes her mother being abused verbally, emotionally, or physically by a man, the only assumptions she can reach are that this is how male/female relationships work, this is the way all women are treated in intimate relationships, and that this is what she, too, can expect from a man when she ventures into a relationship.

The most recent research conducted in the field of domestic violence has shown that children raised in abusive homes experience

- increased rate of death by homicide and suicide
- more depression and emotional injuries, such as low self-esteem
- more aggressive behavior toward others
- high delinquency rates
- poor school adjustment
- higher risk for drug and alcohol use
- earlier marriages and earlier pregnancies
- continuation of violence into adult relationships
- recurring thoughts of homicide toward the batterer in the home
- feelings of needing to protect their mother
- inability to have a "normal" childhood and adolescence
- early learning of denial as a coping mechanism
- taking on roles inappropriate to their age and maturity level
- seeking danger and violence as "normal"
- high risk for child abuse and child sexual assault

If your daughter was raised in a verbally, emotionally, or physically abusive household, she erroneously believes that *this is acceptable behavior.* Since you are her most important role model, as a mother you do not have the option of saying, "Your father treats me this way, but I want better for you." Or, as a father, "I am cruel to your mother. I say vicious things, treat her unbelievably poorly, and knock her around for her own good, but I'll kill a boy who does that to you." Obviously you see the ridiculousness of such comments. They are clearly hypocritical when paired with your actual behavior, and very confusing to a young girl experiencing a romantic relationship. Essentially, what you are saying is, "Do as I say, not as I do."

Take a moment to look at your own relationship(s). Ask yourself the following questions about what goes on in your household:

- Has your daughter witnessed a man calling a woman names, such as "bitch," "whore," "stupid," "ridiculous," and the like?
- Are men considered superior to women? That attitude can be displayed in behaviors that make a woman feel incapable of doing "a man's work," like hovering over her or laughing while she is fixing a car or plumbing or working outside the home. Do men receive preferential treatment?
- Are women the butt of jokes?
- Are women's body parts referred to by vulgar words, such as "tits," "ass," "booty," "cunt," and so on?
- Has a man in your household ever hit, pushed, slapped, grabbed, or restrained a woman?
- Has a man ever exploded in anger and left the house?
- Does the daughter in your home frequently see her mother cry over a difficulty with a man?
- Does the woman in your home remain passive if she has a difference of opinion with a man?
- Does the man usually have the last word?

- Is the daughter told by the mother that it is a woman's obligation to sexually satisfy her man, defer to his judgment, laugh at his jokes, take care of his every need, make herself available to his desires, not complain, suffer through life, "take what you're given," "forgive and forget," treat men like children, be a helpmate, fix whatever is wrong in the relationship?
- Is the daughter or mother told that she's nothing without a man?

If you've answered yes to more than one of these questions, I encourage you to reexamine the relationship model you have given your daughter. If we want our children to replicate our positive behaviors, it stands to reason that they will repeat our negative behaviors as well. If your relationship(s) are not what you desire for your daughter, perhaps you would like to consider relationship or individual counseling, or reading one of the many fine self-help books that are listed in the Resources chapter. If you are in this situation, however, do not tell your daughter, "You're breaking my heart by staying with your boyfriend. Can't you see what he's doing to you? Don't you think you deserve any better?" She could make the same comments to you.

> I couldn't stand to hear my mother and her boyfriend fight. He called her nasty names, and sometimes he would throw things. I could hear my mother crying and pleading. I always had a giant knot in my stomach. Of course, they thought I was sleeping when they fought. I can't believe they would think that, since they were so loud. I'd have to be deaf not to hear them. In the morning, my mom would put on this stupid, grinning face, pretending nothing had happened. I really hated that face.
>
> When I got a boyfriend, I never wanted to go home. I didn't care how he treated me as long as I didn't have to go home to the fighting. My mother was so shocked to find out that my boyfriend wasn't the best choice in the world. How could she even think

that? That guy was her fourth rotten boyfriend, and she used to tell me about how mean my father was. What was she expecting from me?
—ANGELA, SEVENTEEN

ALCOHOL AND DRUG USE

Parental use or abuse of alcohol and drugs is a contributing factor in girls' involvement in abusive relationships. When a young woman sees that the way to relieve stress or escape problems is in a shot glass, a pill (prescribed or illegal), a snort, or a joint, she sees nothing wrong with her boyfriend using the same coping mechanisms. In fact, she feels it is an acceptable choice for her to make when the pressure of her relationship becomes overwhelming.

When a girl's parents use drugs and alcohol, they become emotionally, and perhaps physically, unavailable to her. She learns that her parents are unreliable and that if she has a problem, she must try to solve it on her own. When parents are drunk or high, they may exhibit behaviors they wouldn't if they were sober. This teaches a girl to accept unpredictable behavior in all of her relationships. When parents are substance abusers, a daughter learns to keep the family's shameful secret and is therefore adept at keeping secrets from her parents as well. She also learns that there is something "defective" about her family, which she may translate into "There is something defective in me."

If the father is the substance abuser, the daughter may see the mother endlessly fretting over his out-of-control behavior, repeatedly imploring him to stop using, feeling frustrated, crying, adjusting to his moods, telling the children to do the same ("Let's all be quiet. Daddy has a headache. He doesn't feel good."), feeling responsible for his recovery, or perhaps joining him in his substance abuse.

My dad is a drunk. I can say that now, because I don't pretend that he's not anymore. For a long time I couldn't have friends over and everything revolved around my father's drinking. It was sick. He's really mean when he drinks, so when I was little, I always thought he was mean to me because I was bad. My mother tried to tell me that I wasn't, but he was yelling at her, too, and she felt responsible. When she started drinking with him, that was really the last straw. She was such a hypocrite. Thank God, I have less than a year before I can leave that house. —MOIRA, SEVENTEEN

DEPRESSION AND ANXIETY

Do you or your mate suffer from frequent bouts of depression or anxiety? This is not to be confused with occasional sadness, which we all have from time to time. Depression is different from sadness in many ways. While sadness is transient—it comes and goes, perhaps with a shift in hormones, the seasons, or a particular temporary stressor—by definition, depression lasts most of every day for at least two weeks. In addition, if you are depressed, you have persistent feelings of sadness, anxiety, or emptiness, loss of interest or pleasure in ordinary activities (also called *anhedonia*), and five or more of the following symptoms:

- changes in appetite—either losing your appetite, often resulting in weight loss, or eating ravenously, resulting in weight gain
- sleep problems—insomnia or wanting to sleep all the time
- low energy and feelings of fatigue
- restlessness and irritability
- feelings of worthlessness, hopelessness, or inappropriate guilt
- difficulty thinking, making decisions, or concentrating
- thoughts of death or suicide, or attempts at suicide
- chronic aches and pains that don't respond to treatment
- excessive crying

Anxiety may feel like fear, nervousness, or restlessness with or without a specific reason. Anxiety is actually fear of loss—usually of love, finances, or esteem—in the future.

There are several reasons why a history of depression or anxiety is important to a girl in an abusive relationship. First, children of depressed parents have a significantly higher risk of depression themselves, with girls suffering with the disease two to one over boys. In *Growing Up Sad: Childhood Depression and Its Treatment*, doctors Leon Cytryn and Donald McKnew state that a child's depression is evident in her verbal expressions: she feels hopeless, helpless, worthless, unattractive, unloved, and guilty, and suicidal ideas keep running through her mind.

Second, your daughter's mood and behavior also change when she is in a depressive home: there is a sadness of facial expression and posture, crying, slowness of movement and emotional reactions, disturbance of appetite and sleep, failure in school, increased irritability, and physical complaints for which no physical cause can be found.

When parents are depressed, they can't take care of and nurture a child effectively. They don't have the energy or concentration for the task. When a girl is neglected to some degree, she has fears of abandonment, receives inconsistent parenting, learns to fend for herself, may feel guilty about her parents' sadness, becomes exquisitely attuned to a parent's moods, and usually becomes a rescuer or helper in order to aid the depressed or anxious parent. These are all behaviors that make her a good candidate for an abusive relationship.

The fear of abandonment is acted out in your daughter's relationship when she won't break up with her boyfriend for fear of being alone. He plays on her fears by threatening to leave her or find another girlfriend. Inconsistent parenting leads a girl to feel that she never knows which end is up. Because she grew up in this environment, the chaos of an abusive relationship appears normal to her.

When a girl feels guilty for a parent's sadness, she grows to understand that her boyfriend's feelings are not only her responsibility to fix, they are also her fault. Likewise, because a girl has grown accustomed to anticipating her parent's moods, she now watches her boyfriend's every facial expression and bodily twitch for signs that he may be upset with her, switching to act like the girl he would like, just as she had switched to the daughter her parents would have liked. As previously mentioned, a girl who has been trained to be "a good little helper" now easily brings that rescuer into her relationship with a boy.

> *My mother is depressed a lot of the time. My dad tried to help her but finally gave up and moved out. He wanted to take me with him, but I didn't feel like I could leave my mother. I was sure she'd try to commit suicide if I did. My dad told me that he was sorry, but he deserved to live a better life than he could with my mom, since she wasn't trying to help herself. That was four years ago. She cries a lot and talks about her life being hopeless. She tells me that I am the only bright spot in her life. I guess I am, but you'd never know it by the way she acts. The pressure on me to be perfect all the time is too much. Constantly seeing if she's okay is also too much.*
>
> *The only time I'm happy is when I'm with my boyfriend, who my father can't stand. Dad tells me that he's bad for me and ma-nipulative, just like my mom was to him. My boyfriend lives in a terrible family that's always arguing. He counts on me for his happiness, and I'm not going to let him down.* —ROSA, SIXTEEN

BOUNDARIES

A boundary is a line that marks or fixes a limit. In families, this mark is displayed in the ways each member respects the others as indi-viduals. It also involves the ability to trust and meet one another's needs. In a healthy family there is a boundary between parents and children. There may also be a boundary between the children themselves, with the parents having different expectations of each.

The type of boundaries your family has is important. There are two basic styles of families with regard to boundaries, with most families falling somewhere along the continuum. *Enmeshed* families have very diffuse, blurred, and indistinct boundaries. Parents are too accessible, and their contact with the children may take the form of hovering and invasion of privacy. Because the children are so involved with their parents, they fail to develop independent thinking and behaving, and they don't learn the necessary skills for developing healthy relationships outside the family. While Mom and Dad may be room mom, soccer coach, car-pool driver, and so on, the message a girl in an enmeshed family actually receives is that she is incapable of making good decisions for herself and that she needs someone to take care of her. This type of attitude fosters low self-esteem in a girl and goes on to play out in many areas of her life, including her having an abusive boyfriend.

A *disengaged* family has the opposite dynamics. Here the boundaries are overly rigid, causing each member to function on her own. Interpersonal distance is great, and children do not request support when needed. Communication in a disengaged family is strained and guarded.

> *My parents couldn't care less where I am or what I do. Everyone's in their own little world, and we hardly even talk to each other. There's a lot of stress in my house. I don't know if they would even bat an eyelash if they knew that I had sex for the first time at fourteen and am doing it now with my boyfriend. He's not very nice to me, but it beats being in that house.* —CARLA, FIFTEEN

Sometimes parents are very controlling and don't allow their daughter freedom: freedom of her own thoughts ("What are you thinking about?" "You shouldn't think like that."), freedom of movement ("Where are you going? Who will you be with?"), freedom of expression ("Don't talk like that." "You don't know enough to have that opinion."), and so on. This leaves a girl believing that she can't trust her own thoughts, behaviors, and opinions. She also perceives that having someone control her is normal, possibly even desirable: "My mom and dad act just like my boyfriend, and they love me."

SO NOW WHAT DO YOU DO?

Perhaps some of the family dynamics I have illustrated strike a chord in you. You may have read a few of the descriptions and said to yourself, "That sounds like me," or "That looks like our family." I applaud your honesty and integrity in standing back from your family and looking at it with a critical eye. You have taken a big step in helping your daughter.

So now what do you do? The options depend on the situation. Obviously, remaining in an abusive relationship is highly damaging to children. In most states, this type of atmosphere is categorized as emotional abuse and is cause for Children's Protective Services to investigate the household and possibly remove the children. I urge you to think hard about what you want for your daughter. Will you feel that you have done the best job you can as a mother if your daughter marries an abusive man? A man just like the man with whom you live? As a father, will you feel that you have done the best job you can for your daughter if she marries a man who calls her names, demeans her, hits her, and sexually assaults her? I am sure that the answer is no; otherwise you wouldn't be reading this book.

Now is the time to take decisive action in your own relationship. Individual, couple, and family counseling is available at every income level. I will discuss resources for treatment in the last section of the book; however, please understand that fear of the unknown—in terms of therapy itself or the cost—doesn't need to be a barrier to getting needed help. There are low-cost counseling centers in almost every large city. If you are on a state aid program, consult that office as to resources available to you. If you belong to a place of worship, often parish counseling is offered. For this to succeed, both parents must first be willing to take responsibility for their part in the abusive relationship.

In my private practice, parents usually identify a child as the "problem child" and request that I "fix" her. Therapeutically, this child is known as the identified patient. These parents do not feel that they need treatment, or that family therapy is justified, since it is the specific child who is causing the distress in the household. I may be able to "fix" the child, but then she goes home to her family who has the same behaviors as when the child began therapy. As you have now seen, when your daughter has an abusive boyfriend, the problem may have started in your home. Family therapy, and sometimes private counseling with the girl's parents, is essential.

Just as your daughter's boyfriend has control of his outbursts, you do as well. You *can* stop fighting with your partner in front of your children. You *can* seek help for your discord. Remember, you have control of three things: your own thoughts, your own behavior, and your own reactions (including your reaction to an abusive spouse). At the end of treatment, you may have discovered a way to communicate more effectively and express your anger and disappointment in a different way, raised your self-esteem, and empowered yourself. You may also find that your partner is not willing to change and your relationship may need to end.

If you currently have a drug and/or alcohol problem, now is the best time to enroll in a rehabilitation program, such as a Twelve-Step program (Alcoholics Anonymous, Narcotics Anonymous, and so on), or an inpatient treatment program. The first step to recovery is the willingness to admit your problem and receive help. If your spouse is a user, programs such as Al-Anon are very helpful. You will find information about these in the Resources section at the end of this book.

Depression, anxiety, and other mood difficulties are usually treatable with therapy or a combination of medication and therapy. I encourage you to speak with your family physician about this. While I have addressed the effect that your mood has on your daughter, I am certain that you don't like living this way either. I'm sure you would prefer a happy and complete life as well. It is out there and available if you take a step toward health.

Please remember that just as your daughter is not a victim of her boyfriend's abusive actions, neither are you a victim of drugs or alcohol, depression, or your own abusive relationship. You have made a decision to stay stuck and show your daughter that this is an acceptable way of life.

For your daughter's sake—as well as any other children you may have—I encourage you to be brave and take action today. It is not too late to change, and it is not too late to show your daughter that you can change. It is not too late to become *her* hero.

Sue's Story

Sue was a forty-five-year-old woman I began treating in 1998. She began her relationship with her abusive husband of twenty-four years while they were both in high school. The story of their family dynamics is both interesting and disturbing.

Sue was born in Taiwan and was given to a state orphanage at three weeks of age. Her family already had too many girls. She remained in the orphanage until she was adopted at age four by an Asian-American couple in Southern California. This couple had tried to have children for seven years and finally resigned themselves to the fact that they were infertile.

Sue had only a vague recollection of her time in the orphanage, remembering a feeling of being alone and sad. She recalled her fifth birthday as a happy one and remembered having all of her parents' attention. The next two years were good; then her mother became pregnant. The pregnancy was referred to as a miracle by both of her parents. They were so excited that Sue was thrilled as well. She was looking forward to the baby that she thought would be "hers."

Douglas, the miracle baby, was born to much fanfare and excitement. After his birth Sue's life changed drastically, as she was all but forgotten. Not only did her parents neglect her and focus all of their attention on the baby, but she became something of a Cinderella as well. At the age of seven, she was called upon to do all the housecleaning, laundry, and ironing. Often she came downstairs to find her family eating dinner without calling to her first.

As she and her brother grew, Sue was ignored more and more.

She was an excellent student, studied hard, and earned straight A's. Douglas, on the other hand, was a very poor student but an excellent athlete. Sue's parents were thrilled with his athletic prowess and never missed one of his sporting events. On the other hand, when Sue received academic awards, her parents did not attend. Her teachers found that unusual, as the Asian stereotype included an emphasis on academic achievement, downplaying athleticism.

Sue met Barry in an advanced English class in high school. He wasn't good-looking, but that didn't matter. Barry paid attention to her, and that was good enough for her. On their first date he took her to meet his mother before going to the movies. His father had died when he was twelve, and his mother became an even more dominating force in his life. He was an only child, a second-generation Asian-American, and highly prized by the woman. Sue said he was "incredibly spoiled and could do no wrong."

Sue and Barry went to the same university. She received a partial academic scholarship and paid the remainder of her tuition herself. Although it was out-of-town, her parents and brother never visited her once and didn't really care if she came home for the holidays. She remembers telling her family that she would be home for Christmas. Three Christmas stockings were hanging at the fireplace; hers was not one of them.

Barry was very possessive of Sue's time and attention while at school but would frequently date other women. Even while he was on a date, he called her dorm room to make sure she was staying in for the night. She said she didn't expect him to be faithful to her alone; he was a man and had "needs" she felt she wasn't adequate to fulfill for him in their sexual relationship. She had no desire to date others anyway so was happy to stay in her room and study.

When they married, she felt she was the luckiest girl in the world. Barry was accepted to dental school, and she saw her future as comfortable and assured. She felt fortunate in that he had dated so many other women and ultimately chose her.

They moved in with his mother so that he could attend school. She became a dental assistant with a plan to work for Barry when he graduated. Life with her mother-in-law was predictably difficult. She dictated everything that happened within the family and made no secret of her disdain for Sue. She helped her son in every way, including ironing his underwear. She didn't let Sue cook, telling her that she knew better how to prepare her son's food. Barry refused to have sex with Sue when his mother was home—which was almost always—or when he feared she might come home. As a result, in the three years the couple lived with his mother, Sue recalled that they had sexual relations four times. Each time, it was hurried and unsatisfying for her.

When Barry graduated and opened his dental practice, the couple bought their first home and quickly had a son. Barry was not present at his son's birth, and Sue knew that he was with another woman but never said anything. She was happy to have a baby.

Sue recalled that in the ensuing years her husband verbally demeaned her daily. An fact, he called her many of the same names that her neglectful and cruel parents had used against her: "crazy," "dumb," "ugly," and "idiot." She didn't argue with him and concentrated even more on her son.

Barry's temper frightened Sue. She went out of her way to try to please him so that he wouldn't get angry with her. When he did, she curled up in a ball and hid her head. She dared not ask for any more of his time or attention for fear of angering him. He continued to see other women and demean her talents and abilities.

When her son started kindergarten, Sue began working for Barry as an assistant and bookkeeper. Because she wanted to be home with her son after school, she took her accounting work home, frequently working until two in the morning. Whatever she did was not enough to please her husband, and he criticized her daily.

By the time a former patient referred Sue to me, she was extremely thin and looked far older than her years. Her clothes hung loosely on her body, and I could see that they were quite old. She wore no makeup and looked very tired. She spoke in a low monotone. Her son was now twelve years old. She was being physically and sexually violated by her husband but discounted its severity. She had frequent and urgent suicidal thoughts and felt that it was her "only way out." When I asked her why she didn't merely divorce her husband, she looked at me as though I had asked an odd question.

"I couldn't ever divorce him," she said. "I could never be alone. I couldn't handle it. Anyway, he would take my son and I'd never see him again."

I pointed out the obvious, which was that if she killed herself, she would never see her son again, either, and he would be left with the legacy of a mother who didn't care about him enough to stick around. She was insulted by my statement, and it was good to see her get angry. I asked if her husband had ever threatened to take their son from her, and she said he hadn't but she was sure that would happen. In any case, she reasserted she could not bear to be alone. Of course, she was more alone in her marriage than she would have been living without him, but she was not able to grasp that idea.

Sue continued to come to weekly therapy sessions, although her husband didn't know about the appointments, and I could not call her for fear that he would find out. She didn't tell him because she was sure it would confirm his statements about her being "crazy." In addition, she didn't want the additional wrath of her mother-in-law and knew that she would spread the information throughout the family. As a therapist with a potentially suicidal client, it was very difficult not to be able to contact her.

She didn't have a plan for her suicide, just a vague feeling that it would be better than where she was now; since she wasn't in imminent danger of harming herself, I could not involuntarily admit her to a psychiatric hospital. In the state of California, spousal abuse is not required to be reported to the authorities by a therapist. Thus, I was stuck and didn't know what to do with Sue except listen to her and be available when she wanted to talk.

I still see Sue on a weekly basis. She has not changed her position about not angering her husband, though she now understands that she is being violated in every way. She is willing to accept the abuse as a condition of her marriage.

You can clearly see the ways in which both Sue's and Barry's family dynamics predisposed them to the kind of marriage they have. Sue was essentially told that she was worthless and not treasured by her family. She was told that another person—her brother—was more important than she. It was her job to be quiet, serve the family, and never complain. She was grateful just to have a place to sleep and nothing more. She understood the feeling of abandonment from the time she was an infant and was terrified of that recurring in her life. She did whatever was necessary to make sure she wasn't alone.

Barry, on the other hand, was given unlimited privileges and could do no wrong. He was a male in an Asian household and an only child to boot. His mother doted on him in an unnatural way and taught him, by her example, that women were there to serve him and allow him anything he desired. He was the king.

Unfortunately, by Sue's example, her teenage son has seen how men and women are "supposed" to act in a relationship as well, and he has begun to use the same words his father uses against Sue. Since she has "devoted her life" to the boy, this is heartbreaking to her. Still, she does nothing to change the situation and feels unable to do so. In fact, she feels that perhaps the men are correct about her. She is caught in the middle of wanting to get out of her marriage, fearing being alone, and also fearing losing her son.

11
Girls Who Abuse Boys

WE HAVE already talked about not seeing your daughter as a victim of her abusive boyfriend, that she participates to some degree in the relationship, and the reasons why she may have chosen to stay with him in the face of logic.

In my experience with abusive relationships—both teenage and adult—I see that sometimes a girl is an active participant in her own abuse. If you are a woman, think back for a moment to your own high school years. Do you remember the girls who talked behind your back, tried to steal your boyfriend, and were malicious gossips? Those were emotionally abusive girls. While we know that 97 percent of physical abuse is perpetrated by men and boys, women and girls emotionally abuse others quite often. Your daughter may be an emotional abuser.

This form of abuse may be an act of commission or omission. If your daughter calls her boyfriend names, that is an act of commission. An act of omission might be "forgetting" to pick up her boyfriend when his work shift ends. It may be intentionally harmful or may simply reflect what she has been exposed to in her family relationships. She may actually be provoking abuse, or she may be retaliating against her boyfriend's abuse.

When I lecture in high schools, often boys will come talk to me after class. Some of the comments I hear are:

"My girlfriend goes psycho if I even say hello to another girl. Aren't I allowed to have friends that aren't guys? Sometimes it's a girl I hardly know who's in one of my classes, and I'm just trying to be polite."

"She wants to know where I am all the time. If I'm not with her, she tells me that I must not care about her. She's always trying to make me feel guilty."

"If I don't call my girlfriend at least once every night, she accuses me of not caring about her and starts to cry. I just saw her for half a day at school. Aren't I allowed to have a life?"

"Whenever she wants something from me, she pouts and then cries if she doesn't get it. I can't stand that."

"She tells me what time I should call her or be at her house. If I'm not, she throws a fit."

"She's always crying, but I swear it's not my fault. She's so emotional. I know her parents think she's crying because of me."

"I feel like I'm always apologizing for stuff I didn't do. She tells me I'm looking at girls when I'm not. I love her and I'm not looking at other girls. I can't get her to believe that, so I just end up saying I'm sorry to make her feel better."

Such comments shed a new light on abusive relationships. Who are the abusers in these situations? While none of the boys above were abusers, can you see the ways in which a girl's emotionally abusive behaviors might contribute to her own abuse? As with the actions of an abusive boyfriend, these behaviors stem from feelings of low self-worth and insecurity. Abusive girls attract abusive boyfriends. They play out mutually abusive behavior in their relationships.

As parents, it is important that we do not allow "female privilege" when thinking about the behaviors the boys described. We call it emotional abuse if our daughter's boyfriend does it to her, so why not the reverse? You may think that your daughter is merely re-acting in kind to her boyfriend's abuse or defending herself. That type of reasoning, however, means that abuse is all right as long as it is justified. If this were true, it would be fine for your daughter's boyfriend to hit her if he felt that she was "disrespectful" to him. It would be okay for him to call her a "bitch" if he felt she acted like one. And there would be nothing wrong with his raping her if she wore a short skirt, because "she was asking for it."

> *My girlfriend used to call me a "dick" in front of her friends. It was humiliating. All the girls would laugh and think it was so cute. I told her how I felt and asked her to stop. When she wouldn't, I realized that I was with a girl who told me that she loved me but didn't care anything about my feelings.*
>
> —GREG, EIGHTEEN

Some boys talk in whispers about their girlfriends' unpredictable and volatile temper and the fear it causes in them.

> *Janis used to go off at the least little thing. I never knew what would set her off, so I was always tiptoeing around. One time she threw a plate at my head because I was ten minutes late, and an-other time she grabbed my shirt and yanked all the buttons off be-cause I didn't want to go to the same movie as her.*
>
> —MIKE, SIXTEEN

Boys don't usually report when a girl has physically abused them. They feel that people would make fun of them or joke about their perceived lack of masculinity. They live with the same secre-tiveness and shame that abused girls speak about.

As I've mentioned, girls have the same insecurities as boys; however, a girl's fears are more socially acceptable. Because of their insecurity, they are subject to behaving with many of the same emotionally and verbally abusive behaviors we have discussed ear-lier. Listen to a few more stories I've heard from boys:

When we were in a group, she would tell jokes where the guy was the stooge. The girls would laugh, but one time a male friend of mine said, "What is the deal with male bashing all the time? How come girls are allowed to say whatever they want about guys, but we're called monsters if we say the same sort of things about girls?"

You know what? He was absolutely right. If I told degrading jokes about women, the world would come crashing down around me, but women are always telling the same sort of jokes about men. I don't get it.
—ROB, FIFTEEN

My girlfriend and I both have pagers. Our parents gave them to us so they would know where we are. She pages me nonstop sometimes and expects me to call her back right away. We go to different schools, and she's always thinking that I'm doing something with girls at my school, which isn't true. If I can't call her immediately, she's crying and saying that I couldn't call her back because I was with another girl. I don't know what I have to do to calm her down and get her to stop being so needy.
—ANTHONY, SIXTEEN

She has to be with me all the time. I can't even go anywhere with my own friends if she doesn't come along. All my friends tell me that she's like a parasite and is sucking the life out of me. I don't know what to do. If I'm not with her, she gets hysterical. If I don't start doing some more things by myself with my friends, I'm going to lose them.
—JACK, SIXTEEN

What ever happened to the Golden Rule? I'm sure you have taught your daughter to "do unto others as you would have them do unto you." In every example you've read here, you must ask yourself, "If my daughter were on the receiving end of that behavior, would I think it was acceptable?"

Take a look at the list of behaviors in chapter 6 that might identify a potential abuser. If you suspect that your daughter is exhibiting these warning signs with her boyfriend, show her the list. For example, sometimes girls say, "I love you" too soon as a way of reassuring themselves that boys feel the same way. As I've stated, those three little words are like a giant hook to a girl; she loves to say them, and she loves to hear them.

> *Stacy and I sort of knew each other from church but didn't go to the same school or have any friends in common. She seemed nice, so one day after church I asked her if she wanted to go to a movie the next Friday night. She acted normal at the movie and when we went to Starbucks afterward. I didn't hold her hand or give her a kiss good night because I didn't feel that was right. When I got home that night, there was a message on my answering machine from her. She told me that she thought she was falling in love with me and couldn't wait to see me again. That was too weird. She barely knew me. I didn't take her out again, even though she kept calling me.*
> —RON, SEVENTEEN

Reading books about self-esteem—which are listed in the Resources section—may help your daughter understand her fears, insecurities, and self-doubt. She may discover the roots of her abusive behaviors and decide that she is behaving in an unhealthy manner that certainly won't score her any points with boys. Private counseling may be helpful as well, in which issues of trust, respect (for herself and others), vulnerability, protection, and compassion can be addressed. Your daughter may be ashamed of her actions but not know how to modify them. She may feel helpless and out of control. She may also feel that she is a victim of her moods. Opening up a dialogue with her on this subject could be the gift she needs.

Jana's Story

Jana came in to see me at the request of her mother, who felt her daughter was the "victim" in an abusive relationship. She was fifteen years old, very beautiful, and wise beyond her years.

Both mother and daughter attended the first session. Jana's mother explained that she had been in an extremely abusive marriage with Jana's father. Six years earlier she had taken the girl and her younger brother in the middle of the night, staying at a shelter for victims of domestic violence for one month. Since that time Jana had not had any contact with her father.

Jana spoke of her parents' relationship as "scary" and said that she was happy when they divorced. She said that even though those times were difficult and leaving the family home had been terrible and frightening, she now had great admiration for her mother's decision and strength.

Jana's mother had never remarried but had had two long-term relationships with nice gentlemen. The first had ended because he wanted to marry but she didn't feel she was ready yet. The second relationship dissolved when the man was transferred to the East Coast and Jana's mother didn't want to move her children, feeling they had already endured enough transition in their lives. Jana spoke of both men fondly and said she missed them.

Jana didn't see anything wrong in her relationship with her fifteen-year-old boyfriend, Darren, although her mother said they talked on the telephone several times each night and spent most of their time together, and that Jana cried frequently. She was terribly concerned that her daughter was repeating the cycle of abuse she had seen in her parents' relationship.

In three subsequent individual sessions, it became apparent that the relationship was indeed fairly abusive. However, it was Jana who was the perpetrator. She called Darren several times a day to make sure he was where he said he was going to be. She became very jealous if he so much as glanced at another girl at school, even if the girl was a friend. She accused him endlessly of wanting to be with someone else and called him unkind names like "cream puff" and "baboon" to make him feel insecure.

Jana cried frequently, as her mother had reported, but it was because Darren was trying to assert himself, asking her to stop calling him so often to check up on him. He told her that he loved her and didn't think of being with other girls. She demanded that he tell her that he loved her many times a day and had been the first to say it—on their very first date.

I pointed out her abusive behaviors and suggested that perhaps she behaved that way because she wanted to ensure that he wouldn't leave her, as her father and her mother's two boyfriends had done. Since those experiences were beyond her control, she felt that she must enforce control over this relationship due to her own fears and insecurities.

Jana understood those concepts and felt ashamed of her behaviors. I assured her that a loving relationship did not include control but allowed both partners to be free to do as they chose. If they loved each other, they did not exhibit hurtful behaviors. By acting the way she did with Darren, she couldn't know whether he was with her because of fear and intimidation or because he truly cared for her. In any case, she was certainly ensuring that he would eventually want to leave the relationship because he was tired of her disrespect.

After Jana was able to explain what she was doing and why, we shifted the course of our treatment to resolving her issues of poor self-esteem, fear of abandonment, the resentment she had because her mother remained in a violent marriage, the true and unexpressed grief she felt over losing her mother's boyfriends, and fear of her own future with men.

Why Teens Don't Tell

12

How to Talk to Your Daughter About Abuse

YOU HAVE TAUGHT your daughter that she can talk with you about anything. You listened to her fears of a monster in her closet. You reassured her that she would be fine on her first day of kindergarten. You commiserated when her best friend decided not to be her best friend anymore because she liked the new girl in class better. Now, when she is facing the most frightening and confusing situation in her life, why won't she talk with you?

> We used to have such a close relationship. We talked about anything and everything. Her mother died when she was seven, so I've been both mom and dad to her ever since. I talked with her about the facts of life, and I was the first person she talked to when she got her period. She wasn't embarrassed or uncomfortable. We even went out for ice cream to celebrate her entrance into womanhood.
>
> First, I don't understand how she got herself involved with her creep of a boyfriend. But really, I just want to be able to talk with

her about it. I don't know if she's in trouble. I don't know if he's hurting her. I don't know if they're having sex. She cries a lot but won't tell me what it's about. Ever since he came along, I feel like I'm locked out of her life.

In the beginning I had to check my own thoughts about him to see if I was jealous that a new man was in her life, sort of taking my place. He seemed like a nice-enough kid the first couple of times I saw him. Then she started going downhill emotionally. She stopped showing me her report cards after two months, and I had to get them directly from the school. Her grades had dropped.

I try and try to talk to her about him, but she just gets defensive and tells me that I don't know anything about him. I know she's torn: she wants our relationship back, but she wants to hold on to him. I don't know how to reach her. —CARL, FORTY-SEVEN

You may have experienced the same concern and frustration. Parents frequently ask, "Where did my daughter go?" All of a sudden she's turned into someone you barely recognize and with whom you can't communicate. She has shut you out of her life.

Teenage girls don't talk with their parents about their abusive relationships for many reasons. Let's examine them.

She has trouble identifying her relationship as abusive

In chapter 2 we discussed abusive emotional and verbal behaviors that are frequently overlooked. Show her the various checklists in this book. They may well have a profound effect on the way she views her relationship. Until this time, she may not have thought she had a problem, so why should she talk with you about it?

It is important for her to be in a relationship

The peer pressure in high schools is intense. One of the cardinal rules is: If you don't have a boyfriend, there's something terribly wrong with you. Some girls will do almost anything to hold on to their boyfriend, even suffer through an abusive relationship.

She believes that jealousy and possessiveness are synonymous with love

Because of your daughter's lack of dating experience, she may feel that if her boyfriend tells her not to look at other boys, it really means that he loves her. She may also believe that his wanting to spend every moment with her as well as needing to know where she is at all times is the ultimate in romance.

She sees violence at home

As I detailed in chapter 10, if your home is a violent environment, she may think it acceptable for a boy to yell at her, hit her, call her names, and generally abuse her. How can she ask you for advice when you are in the same situation she is? What will you tell her: "Do as I say, not as I do"? Because she has seen that you cannot manage your own life effectively, she sees no point in talking with you about her relationship, and quite possibly she doesn't want to distress you further with another problem.

She is afraid

Often an abusive boyfriend will make threats such as "If you break up with me, I'll beat up your little brother." "I'll tell everyone that you're a slut." "I'll kill your dog." "I'll kill myself." "You won't know when, but I'll get you for this." Someone who would make these statements is obviously a very disturbed young man. Because of his abusive behavior, a girl has every reason to believe his threats . . . and so do you. In fact, 75 percent of abused women who are killed by their abusers are killed when they attempt to leave the relationship.

She doesn't want you to think she has poor judgment

See it through her eyes: just when she has implored you to trust her, she makes a poor choice in a boyfriend. Because she is a teenager, and because she is your daughter, she doesn't want to look foolish.

She doesn't want to lose her freedom

You may place stricter curfews or implement tighter controls over her behavior when she is out with her abusive boyfriend in order to protect her. To forestall this, she stops communicating with you. She knows that when she tells you she is going out with her female friends, you may think that she is really going to meet her boyfriend, and perhaps she is. You doubt her, and so you lay down the law more strictly than you did before she started seeing her boyfriend.

She doesn't want to be pressured into breaking up with her boyfriend

She knows how you feel about him. If she gives you even more evidence of his poor behavior, you may forbid her to see him, and that would be unbearable. She faces the dilemma of choosing between her boyfriend and her parents. Don't give her that ultimatum unless you are prepared for consequences you may not like. I have spoken with countless parents who are heartbroken that their daughters left home to live with their abusive boyfriends. They don't know how to get them back, especially if they are eighteen and therefore legal adults.

She feels guilty

If she is sexually active, she may feel true remorse but be too ashamed and afraid to tell you. When a young client of mine contracted a sexually transmitted disease from her abusive boyfriend, she was terrified to tell her parents but understood that she needed medical attention. She brought them into my office to break the news to them. They'd had no idea she was sexually active. After telling them of her infection, she tearfully begged, "Please don't hate me. I love you. I'm so sorry." If she is using drugs or alcohol, she will naturally be frightened to tell you about her use, as it is illegal and she correctly fears your disapproval.

OPENING A CONVERSATION

Before you talk with your daughter, pay close attention to your own feelings and biases toward her relationship with the abusive boyfriend, then leave them outside the discussion. Of course you want her to break up with him, but in opening up a conversation with your daughter, it is not wise to start by maligning him. The conversation will end instantly.

I feel that the best way to approach this difficult situation is to start a dialogue rather than an interrogation. She may feel overwhelmed, and quite frankly, you may not truly want to know every detail of the relationship, especially if sexual activity is involved. Try an opener such as, "I've noticed that you look sad lately. Why don't we talk about it? I'd like to help." That is an invitation to a conversation that lets her know you are not only concerned, but you care about what she has to say.

Notice, too, that there aren't any yes or no questions in the example above. When you ask open-ended questions, you ask her to join in the conversation. Teenagers are notorious for giving monosyllabic answers so that they don't have to converse with parents who, in their eyes, couldn't possibly understand them.

Let your daughter know that you are not going to insist that she break up with her boyfriend. This will allow her to speak with you more honestly, since that is her biggest fear. Yes, I know that you want her to end her relationship. When you follow the exercises and suggestions in this book with your daughter, she may come to the same conclusion without your insistence. Normally, a teenage girl will rebel against her parents' wishes, even if she knows they are right. It is part of proving her independence. Do you remember when she was four years old and her favorite word was *no*? You could ask her if she wants a cookie or a new Barbie, and her answer would still be no. At that age, one of a child's tasks is to develop a sense of autonomy and independence from her parents. It is often referred to as "the first adolescence."

In her teenage years she is attempting the same task. You want her to make the decision to leave her boyfriend herself. In this way she will not have been forced, and she also will see that she can make important decisions wisely. After all, that is one of our chief jobs as parents: to teach our children to leave us knowing how to make good decisions on their own.

It is important for your daughter to know that you are on the same team as her in this matter. You want to do whatever is beneficial to her emotional health and safety. It is also critical to assess whether legal or medical attention is warranted. If so, the Resources section at the end of this book can help guide you.

Listen nonjudgmentally, even if she tells you how wonderful he is. Do not roll your eyes or grimace. You have invited her to speak honestly with you, so don't inhibit her with facial expressions or by interrupting her thoughts. Empathic comments such as, "I can understand how you must feel" or "That sounds like it was very difficult for you to handle" help her identify her own confused feelings while showing her that you are on her side.

In initial conversations, your job is to listen, reflect back that you understand what she is saying, and let her know you are available for future discussions. Later in this process, you can enlist her compassion for your opinion by using "I statements." This is how it is done: "I feel_____when you_____because_____." An example might be: "I feel helpless when you shut me out because I love you so much." In a simple sentence, you have told her about the emotion you are feeling, the action she took, and why you feel that way. Notice that it starts with "I" rather than "you." Starting with "you"—"you never listen to me"—creates a defensive posture in your daughter. She must fight back and rebel.

Do not expect her to come forth with her entire sad story during the first conversation. Likewise, don't even expect her to talk with you right off the bat. She needs to test you out and see if your actions fit your words. She will have to see that you care about her in other ways. Teenagers are constantly testing their parents' words and actions for authenticity. In this case, you can tell yourself that life is about *evolution* rather than *revolution*. Don't expect her to change overnight. Her development into a woman happens in baby steps. You will need to have several conversations with your daughter before she truly understands the points I'm making here. It may take a while for her to trust you, but in the process all of you will learn and grow.

Above all, you want to be your daughter's safe place to fall. She needs to know that she will always be welcomed at home. I have told my children, "If you committed a terrible crime, I would hate that you did it, but I would never hate you. If you went to prison in Poughkeepsie, I would sell our house and buy one in Poughkeepsie so that I could visit you every day. There is nothing you can do that will keep me from loving you." Your daughter needs to know that her mom and dad still love her and will take her back, no matter what she's done.

Susan's Story

I spoke to Susan's high school psychology class in early 1999. While I lecture, I make note of the girls who look down at their desks and can't meet my eyes, or those who silently cry. I know they are in trouble. Susan showed both of those signs. I was glad when she asked to speak with me after class, which was the last period of the day. We went to a quiet part of the school library and she spoke softly so that no one would hear her.

"I really want to talk to you, but do you promise not to tell my parents?" she asked.

"Well, I'm mandated to report child abuse and also if you are going to harm yourself or someone else," I said. "If any of that is present in your life and you don't want me to tell your parents, the police, or Children's Protective Services, you shouldn't tell me anything. If that is not the case, I will not talk with your parents and you can trust me. Are you in some kind of trouble with your boyfriend, honey?"

Susan began to cry again. I put my arm around her shoulder and let her cry until she decided to stop.

"I don't know what to do. He's so mean to me. I want to talk to my parents about it, but I can't."

"Why is that?" I asked. "What will happen?"

"My household is a little weird. I mean, I love my parents and everything, but I can't really go to them with any problems. They don't have such a great marriage, and my mom is depressed a lot. My dad is really strict. It's like I don't want to add to my mom's worries, and I'm afraid that my dad would never trust me again, or he'd go beat up Sam."

"I can certainly understand the predicament you're in. Do you want to tell me what's going on with your boyfriend? I'm not your mom, but I am a mom and maybe I can help a little," I offered.

Susan began to cry again. "He was so nice to me when we first started going together about five months ago. He was so sweet and would call me, bring me little gifts, and compliment me all the time. But as soon as I told him that I loved him, it all started going downhill. He told me he loved me first, though. So it's not like I said it and it scared him off."

"How long after you began dating did he tell you that he loved you?"

"On the third date. We had gone to a romantic movie, *Message in a Bottle,* and afterward he said it to me. I was really happy and told him that I felt the same way about him."

"Susan, love takes time and shared experiences to develop. How much did you know about Sam on the third date?"

"Not much," she replied glumly. "I feel so stupid. I guess I just wanted to know what it was like to be in love and to have a boy love me. I know my parents love me, but I don't think they love each other. At least they don't act like they do. Until I met Sam, I thought that was my destiny, too."

"That's understandable. Everyone wants to be loved and accepted. You don't need to feel stupid about that. Why can't you talk to your parents about this?"

"My mom cries a lot, especially after my dad yells at her or calls her names. Sometimes I really hate him for it, but then I feel guilty for feeling that way. I heard her on the phone one time when she was talking to her sister. She said, 'If I could get out of here and away from him, I would. But I can't disturb Susan's life and make her move when she's in high school, and I won't leave her here with him. I feel like an animal in a cage.' I can't tell you how much that hurt me. So you can see why I can't talk to my mom about anything bad."

"I sure can. It must be difficult for you to live in that house sometimes."

"It is, and my dad is so strict with me. He doesn't give me any room to move. I really had to beg him to let me go out with Sam just to dinner or a movie. I'm sixteen, and he just raised my curfew to eleven P.M. on the weekends. Everyone else has at least a midnight curfew, but you don't argue with my dad. If you do, the roof will fall in. I mean, he doesn't hit me, but he's got a look that terrifies me. I don't want him to give me that look. Anyway, if I told him what was going on with Sam, he'd never let me out of the house again, and he'd never let me forget what a screwup I am."

"Wow, that's tough. Exactly what is going on with Sam?" I asked.

"He's always trying to make me feel bad about myself. He criticizes me all the time, and it seems like anything that happens to him is my fault. I don't know, maybe it is. I don't feel like I know anything anymore. He calls me names in front of other people and then laughs at me if I get upset. He'll say stuff like, 'Oh, are you on the rag, honey?' It's so rude and it humiliates me. I've tried to tell him that, but he just laughs at me even more and tells me I don't know how to take a joke."

"So, he's verbally and emotionally abusive," I said.

"Yeah, and there's another thing," she said slowly, looking down at the library table. "I might be pregnant. I'm three days late and I'm petrified." She started crying again. "If my father knew I was having sex, he'd send me away to a girl's boarding school and do something terrible to Sam. He's the type of guy who holds grudges. If he ever spoke to me again, he'd never let me forget it.

He'd make me have the baby, away from my mother, and give it up for adoption."

Susan was in a bad spot. She came from a household with a history of domestic violence, her mother was depressed, and her father was abusive, overly controlling, and unreasonable. In addition, she felt tremendous guilt because, in her mind, she was the reason her mother couldn't escape her abusive environment. You can see why she couldn't go to her parents in a time of trouble. She didn't feel welcome in her own home. Add that to the stress of an abusive boyfriend and a fear of being pregnant, and Susan was ready to crack.

I asked her if she would feel comfortable talking with the school counselor. I told her that I had become well acquainted with the woman and thought very highly of her. She was kind and nonjudgmental, and I thought she could help. She asked if I would go with her, which I did.

Susan spoke very candidly with the counselor, as she had with me. I then left the situation, knowing she was in such good hands. Susan took a pregnancy test and, to her relief, found that she wasn't pregnant. She continued to see the counselor regularly and in a short time was able to break away from Sam. She is planning to go away to college, which is a good idea for both her and her mother.

Girls need someone to talk to who won't judge them. Naturally, as her parents you hope that she can come to you. I think it is always a good idea to let kids know other trusted people they can turn to in a time of difficulty, if they don't feel they can come to you: a member of the clergy, a school counselor, or any other nonjudgmental and objective third party.

13

Medical, Legal, and Psychological Interventions

Confronting Abuse

LET'S SAY THAT, although you have repeatedly spoken to your daughter in the manner described in chapter 12, she hasn't ended or modified her relationship with her abusive boyfriend. The time for talk is over. Now is the time to get outside help. There are other actions you can take on her behalf if you still fear for her emotional and physical safety.

MEDICAL HELP

If your daughter has been physically or sexually assaulted, it is imperative that she receives immediate medical assistance. Please do not judge whether you think she needs help or not; sometimes blunt trauma to the head is not visible, and certainly internal injuries aren't either. You may not know that a bone is broken until X rays are taken. Because she wants to protect her boyfriend, she may tell you the injuries aren't bad or don't hurt. Understand that this is another example of denial. Take your daughter to the emergency room of your nearest hospital.

Your first instinct may be to call the police. However, her medical safety is the primary order of concern. While she is at the hospital, a member of the staff will call the police for you, they will come to the hospital, and you can then file a report.

If your daughter was sexually assaulted—raped—by her boyfriend, emergency room personnel follow a procedure designed to best help the patient. First, a nurse will assess whether she is medically stable: is she bleeding, has she been shot, stabbed, tortured, or strangled, or are any other injuries visible that need immediate attention? While this is happening, the police are called. If your daughter is not deemed medically stable, treating those injuries will come before sexual assault is assessed and dealt with.

When she is medically stable, the police will interview her and file a report. After that, a doctor or nurse will conduct a full-body examination. This includes blood pressure, respiratory check, and visual examination of the entire body. Next, a gynecological exam will be conducted. This will undoubtedly be very difficult for your daughter. Please assure her that the examiner is very careful and professional and that only the necessary number of people are in the room. It will not take long.

During the exam, a doctor will examine the cervix and vagina. Semen samples will be taken, possibly for DNA testing. Swabs will be used to take cultures for testing of sexually transmitted diseases. Your daughter's pubic hair will be cut and combed, in an effort to search for evidence. Tissue samples of material under the fingernails may be requested, as well as photographs of your daughter's body. At this time, the doctor usually makes a precautionary assumption of possible pregnancy and sexually transmitted diseases. To that end, your daughter may be given the morning-after pill and injections of antibiotics to help ward off gonorrhea and chlamydia. Blood will also be drawn for tests for hepatitis B and HIV.

Last, the staff or police officer may assign a social worker to your case to help support the girl and her family. A list of rape-crisis hot lines and local support groups will also be given.

In the case of physical assault—without sexual assault—the doctors follow much of the same protocol: a whole-body examination is conducted to test for any threatening injuries, treatment occurs, and the police are called. Doctors also want to ensure that the patient wasn't raped as well. Experts have told me that sometimes when they see a girl who was both raped and physically assaulted, she claims not to have been raped. This may be due to shame, fear—of the boy or her parents—and not wanting the police to question her boyfriend and parents.

Can minors receive medical attention without parental consent? The laws may be different in your state; however, the doctors with whom I spoke agreed that treating the patient comes first. They attempt to reach a parent whenever possible. If the girl insists that her parents not be called, they will attempt to assess the reason. In any case, they will treat the child and worry about legalities later. "The legal part is not our job," said one doctor. "We are here to help those who are injured or sick. If a parent is going to sue me, I guess I'd have to deal with it when it came up. Meanwhile, I'd hope that they were grateful that their daughter got the medical attention she needed."

LEGAL HELP

There are variations from state to state about the ways in which minors are protected under the law against abusive boyfriends. Because I can only state generalities, please check my information with your local police department, legal clinic, or lawyer.

Dating abuse is, for legal purposes, considered another classification of domestic violence. Parents of girls in abusive relationships have legal options for protecting their daughter. Please understand that all the suggestions I'm giving you are of less value if your daughter denies the abuse or refuses to leave the relationship.

If your daughter comes home and says that she feels threatened by her boyfriend, call the police. These may be actual verbal threats to her safety or threats against her family or friends. He may also be using threatening behavior, such as wielding a weapon or stalking her. Assuming there has been no abusive physical contact—in which case you would take her to the emergency room first—you can make a police report, also called an incident report.

Make sure to get the police officer's name and the report number. Even if your daughter pleads with you not to do so, it is important that you file the report because there will be a paper trail in case of future abusive behavior. The police will be able to see that her boyfriend has a history or pattern of abusive behaviors. There may not be enough evidence at this time for the police to take action; then again, they may go to his house and talk with him and his parents and say enough to scare him, or they might actually bring him to the police station for a while.

Another benefit of calling the police is that you may be able to ask for an **emergency protective order (EPO),** also referred to as a restraining order. Margaret Bayston, the legal-services director for Laura's House, a shelter for victims of domestic violence, explained the three different types of restraining orders that you can request for your daughter.

You can request an EPO on the spot from a police officer. It can specify that your daughter's boyfriend stay a certain distance away from her—usually one hundred yards—and that he not contact her in any way. To qualify for an EPO, you must present that your daughter is in immediate and present danger of violence. This is evidenced by a recent incident or threat of abuse. The EPO takes effect when the abuser is served. This is taken care of by the police if the boyfriend can be found. If they can't find him immediately, you will want to have someone else hand it to him.

The EPO is only valid for five business days or seven calendar days. This gives you enough time to file for a **temporary restraining order (TRO).**

There is no fee for an EPO. The EPO should be kept on your daughter's person at all times. If her boyfriend continues to harass her and she must call the police, an officer will ask to see her copy before he can take action. You can keep a copy and give another copy to her school officials. You must attach a copy to your application for a TRO. Remember: you only have a few days of some sort of protection with an EPO, so applying for a TRO is essential if you feel that your daughter is still in danger.

A TRO is a domestic-violence restraining order issued by a judge. With it, your daughter's boyfriend cannot contact her by phone, letter, or e-mail, or molest, strike, attack, threaten, sexually assault, and otherwise disturb your daughter's peace. It will also order that he stay a specified distance away from her at all times—usually one hundred yards. Often, if the charge is stalking, the abuser may be ordered to stay three hundred yards from your daughter, and you can get a permanent restraining order that can last up to ten years.

The TRO may also direct the abuser to reimburse you for any out-of-pocket expenses that were a direct cause of the domestic violence. These costs may be medical bills, the cost to fix a window he smashed, and so on. He also may be ordered to return your daughter's personal property. In California, domestic-violence abusers are also mandated to attend a yearlong batterer's treatment program and present the judge with a certificate of completion. The state of California also mandates that the woman or girl taking out the TRO must attend a ten-week personal empowerment program (PEP).

The TRO lasts approximately three weeks, and there is no fee involved. Many legal clinics, lawyers, and justice centers can help you obtain a TRO. Your police department will give you information about agencies that will assist and file for you. Your daughter's boyfriend must be notified of the TRO hearing a minimum of four hours in advance. He may come to the hearing if he wants to.

Your daughter is eligible for a TRO under the following circumstances:

- Her boyfriend assaulted or attempted to assault her or another member of her family.
- He caused, threatened, or attempted bodily injury to her or another member of her household.

- He made her or a member of her household afraid that he would commit physical or emotional harm to them.
- He sexually assaulted or attempted to sexually assault her or a member of her household.
- He stalked her.

If you would like protection for more than three weeks, the next step to take is an **order to show cause (OSC), or permanent restraining order.** The date of the OSC hearing before a judge is generally decided at the time of receipt of the TRO, so you have plenty of notice should you want to gather evidence of the boyfriend's abuse, alter your work schedule, and so on. The OSC is in effect for three years, with many of the same restrictions as the TRO; however, it may be modified to read "no violent contact" rather than no contact at all. You or your daughter may request that a no-contact order stay in effect if you feel it is warranted. When there is an OSC, the boyfriend has fourteen days' notice so that he has the opportunity to come to court and explain his side of the story, if he so desires.

The permanent restraining order stays in effect for three years unless your daughter goes back to court and requests to have it removed. Tearing up the copy does not remove the restraining order. As with the TRO, she should keep a copy on her at all times; also give a copy to her school officials and whoever else you feel will be with your daughter a good portion of the day.

Break the Cycle, a wonderful organization that helps both girls in abusive relationships and their parents, has put together several sheets of information about restraining orders. (See how you can contact them in the Resources section at the end of the book.) Break the Cycle clearly delineates what a restraining order *will not do* for you and your daughter. It will not

- guarantee her personal safety
- guarantee that the abuser will not still be able to intimidate or scare her

- guarantee that the abuser will not come back
- guarantee that the abuser will be out of her life
- guarantee that the abuser will not destroy property that may be irreplaceable
- "cure" the abuser
- act as a bulletproof shield

Many parents find that it is very difficult to obtain a restraining order for their daughter against her wishes. You may see that she is in danger, but she may still be in the denial stage, thinking that her boyfriend would never hurt her, you just don't like him, and so on. This becomes a tricky issue for several reasons. Although you can obtain a restraining order without her approval, you cannot force her to enforce it. In other words, you may have a TRO against her boyfriend, but she may continue to date him when you're not around. In that case, the TRO is something of a sham.

Break the Cycle explains another reason that getting a TRO without your daughter's consent is difficult. They feel that doing so replaces the boyfriend's control over the girl with her parents' control. They think that the girl must be allowed to make her own decision, thereby taking back her own control and power. While I agree with that principle wholeheartedly, I also think that as her parents, you may have better judgment than she does, since you are not romantically involved. In addition, if your daughter is being physically or sexually assaulted, you must protect her the best you can, even if she doesn't want your protection. Naturally, you would like her to reach that conclusion herself, but in some cases a girl might be dead or seriously injured first.

Bear in mind that if you give her school officials a copy of a TRO, they can call the police if he makes contact with your daughter on school property. Likewise, if a neighbor has a copy, she can call the police if the boyfriend is seen on your property. But it will be difficult to enforce if your daughter's boyfriend attends her school. Most schools today are so overcrowded that it would be next to impossible for anyone to keep an eye on just one child. How can one keep the boy from bumping into your daughter, talking to her in passing, and so on? What happens if he is in one of her classes? You *are* able to request that her boyfriend be moved to another class. Sometimes a judge will order that the boyfriend transfer to another school because he understands the difficulty in enforcing the restraining order while the teens attend the same school.

It is vital to contact the police each and every time the TRO is violated, not only because it establishes a history of violations but also because when a court order is violated and not enforced, it gives the abusive boyfriend a feeling of great power and control. He thinks that not even the law can stop him from harassing your daughter.

What happens if your daughter's boyfriend violates the restraining order—that is, he contacts her in some way when ordered not to? Laws are different in many states, but if he is a minor, he may be arrested and taken to juvenile hall. If he is a legal adult—eighteen in most states—he may be taken to jail. Detention sentences are at the discretion of a presiding judge who takes into account the boyfriend's past *reported* abusive behaviors. If he sees that there is a history of abuse on the part of the boy, the detention may be longer than if there is no prior reported history.

It is very important that you and your daughter create a safety plan for her in the event that her boyfriend continues to make abusive contact. I have included on the following pages a personalized safety plan. I urge you to go over it with your daughter.

PERSONALIZED SAFETY PLAN FOR TEENS

The following steps represent my plan for increasing my safety and preparing in advance for the possibility of further violence. Although I do not have control over my partner's violence, I do have a choice about how to respond to him and how to best get myself to safety.

SAFETY DURING AN ARGUMENT

1. If we have an argument on a date and I feel unsafe, I will
    _____
    _____. (Who could you
    call to get a safe ride home? What would you do if left in an iso-
    lated area?)

2. If we have an argument at school and I feel unsafe, I will
    _____
    _____. (Who could help you? Where
    could you be safe at school? What teacher/counselor do you
    trust?)

3. If we have an argument at a house and I feel unsafe, I will try
    to have us discuss it in _____.
    (Try to avoid arguments in the bathroom, garage, or kitchen,
    near weapons, or in rooms without access to a door.)

4. I will use _____ as my code word with my family and
    friends so that they will know to call for help.

SAFETY IN MY HOME

1. I will _____
    if he comes over and I'm alone and feeling unsafe. (Who can
    you call to come over? Who can you call if you need help?)

2. I will _____
    if we get into an argument and I feel unsafe. (What exits are
    there in your house? Where are all the phones that you can use
    to call the police?)

3. When he calls and I feel threatened, I will _____
    _____
    _____. (Can you screen
    your calls with an answering machine? Change your phone

number? Could you have the phone company trace the calls for a stalking report?)

4. If I see him standing outside I will _____

    _____

    _____ so that I can be safe. (Who can help you? Can you take pictures or document how many times it happens, in order to help you file a stalking report?)

Steps for Parents

In addition, here are some other valuable safety tips for your daughter:

- Tell as many people as possible that the relationship was abusive and is now over. Ask them to look out for your daughter when you are not with her and call the police if they see him with her. Ask your daughter to do the same with her friends. If she doesn't want to, then you must do it for her. Abuse is often a dark secret. Bringing it out into the light gives it less power.
- The preceeding safety plan will help your daughter escape if she is alone in your house with him. Practice it with her.
- Urge her not to be alone in isolated areas.
- Ask her school counselor if she knows of any dating-violence support groups, and encourage your daughter to join. There is comfort in shared experiences. As with most support groups, the members are less likely to return to their former behavior.
- Tell her to trust her instincts. If she feels fearful, there is a good reason. Unlike the feelings she denied while in her abusive relationship, her instincts are probably very sound. Fear is a wonderful warning bell that clues us in

ahead of time that something is wrong. Encourage her to listen to her fears and act appropriately.

PSYCHOLOGICAL HELP

Your daughter may have been through a harrowing experience with her abusive boyfriend. His verbal and emotional abuse may have left her feeling demeaned and shaken and destroyed her self-confidence and self-respect. In addition, if she was physically or sexually violated, she may have bruises or scars or perhaps has had to undergo surgery. Feelings of shame, guilt, and self-loathing are common.

Quite often a girl feels personally responsible for putting her boyfriend in jail if he violated his restraining order. This is a good opportunity to remind her that everyone has free will and can make choices accordingly. Just as it was his choice to abuse her, it was again his choice to violate the law. His jail time is a natural consequence of his lack of regard for the law. Understanding what would happen to him if he violated the TRO, he knowingly and with free will chose to ignore the law. His lack of judgment is not her fault.

One ramification of having been in a highly abusive relationship is a little-considered psychological difficulty known as **post-traumatic stress disorder (PTSD).** You may associate this malady with war veterans or victims of torture. PTSD is an authentic diagnostic category that all therapists recognize. In my experience dealing with abused women and girls, most of them exhibited some or many symptoms of PTSD. This description includes a partial list of the criteria:

The person has been exposed to a traumatic event in which both of the following were present: (1) The person experienced, witnessed, or was confronted with an event or events that involved actual or threatened death or serious injury, or a threat to the physical integrity of self or others; (2) the person's response involved intense fear, helplessness, or horror.

You can see how your daughter's abusive relationship falls into this category. Symptoms of PTSD are displayed in a variety of ways:

- intrusive and distressing recollections of the abuse
- nightmares
- feeling like the abuse is recurring, in the form of flash-backs
- efforts to avoid thoughts, feelings, or conversations about the abuse
- efforts to avoid activities, places, or people that bring up recollections of the abuse
- inability to remember important aspects of the abuse
- diminished interest or participation in significant activities (graduation ceremony, prom, family reunion, or vacations)
- inability to have a full range of feelings
- detachment or estrangement from loved ones or friends
- a sense of a foreshortened future (doesn't expect to marry, have children, or have a normal life span)
- difficulty falling or staying asleep
- irritability or outbursts of anger
- difficulty concentrating
- hypervigilance (always looking over her shoulder, checking things out)
- exaggerated startle response (jumps when someone claps or a door is slammed)

If your daughter has exhibited many of the behaviors above, I encourage you to seek therapeutic help for her. As parents, we often think that once a traumatic situation is over, our children will be fine. After all, we feel, it was just a high school romance, the guy was a creep, and good riddance to him. She should be thrilled that he's out of her life! Most often, however, that is not the way your daughter feels. She was in love with her boyfriend. She has many confused but intense feelings wrapped up in her relationship with him. As parents, it is vital that we are sensitive to those feelings, even if we don't understand or agree with them. They are her feelings, after all, and she is entitled to them.

As parents, we would also like to think that because we love our children so deeply, we are able to fix all of their problems. This is simply not the case. Perhaps we don't have the knowledge or expertise. We may be too personally involved to be objective. We often allow feelings to obstruct thoughts. Those are some of the reasons that seeking professional therapy would be beneficial for your daughter—and also for your family.

Many people still believe that counseling is only for "crazy" people, or that people who can't solve their problems on their own are "weak." They worry that others will judge them in this way as well. But I believe that everyone can benefit from having a non-prejudicial third party to speak with from time to time. We all have moments in our lives when we could use a little help. This is one of those times. Do not let fear prevent you from seeking the very best help you can get for your daughter at this crucial time.

PTSD rarely goes away by itself. Some of the symptoms may lessen in time, but without professional help, many get pushed back and reappear at other times that may or may not be related to her former abusive relationship.

Family therapy is also valuable because you went through the trauma together. Also, as mentioned in chapter 10, this may be an excellent opportunity to improve your family as a team. A therapist's office is a safe environment where you can express true and deep feelings for one another—perhaps things you've held in for a long time. The therapist can offer suggestions or exercises to make changes for the family and make it stronger. Please don't pass up this unique opportunity because of preconceived ideas about counseling.

Sometimes expense is a deterrent to getting help. Most people believe that therapy is very costly. That is not always the case. Help is available to those in every income bracket, and I have listed ideas for you to consider in the Resources section at the end of this book.

In general, look for a therapist with an expertise in family counseling. They often have the initials MFCC (Marriage, Family, and Child Counseling) or MFT (Marriage and Family Therapy) after their names. You want to inquire whether they treat many teenagers and if they have a good knowledge of domestic violence. This is important. Not every counselor handles many teens or domestic-violence cases; those who don't may not understand the difficulties your daughter, and the entire family, has faced.

If after exploring the options therapy still seems too costly to you, consider the cost that your daughter may pay if she does not receive help at this time.

Laura's Story

Laura came into my office with her mother, who was concerned for her entire family's safety. Laura had just broken up with an abusive boyfriend, and he didn't take it well. He broke off the driver's-side mirror on her car and removed her rear license plate, apparently hoping she would attract the attention of the police. He also began stalking her and making threats to the family.

Laura and her mother were panicked. "He's a real head case," Laura said. "I don't know what he's capable of. He always told me that if I ever broke up with him, I'd regret it."

I asked Laura's mother if she and her husband had spoken with the boy about these incidents. She said that they were too frightened of him to do so. I asked if they had spoken with his parents.

"The apple doesn't fall far from the tree in his family," Laura explained. "His father is a real creep, and his mother has this attitude that 'boys will be boys' and defends everything her darling son does. She doesn't know the half of it, but even if she did, it wouldn't make a difference and it would just make him more angry."

"Have you reported any of these incidents to the police?" I asked.

"Yes, but I didn't have any evidence so they couldn't do anything," Laura said. "They just told me to be careful."

I advised them to look into obtaining a restraining order against the boy and told them how to do it.

"Wouldn't that just make him more psycho?" Laura asked. "I mean, he doesn't like to be told what to do, and he doesn't think anyone should stop him."

"I'm sure that's true in his mind, but that's not true in the eyes of the law," I answered. This is a common fear of women in abusive relationships. They are afraid to further anger the abuser and worry that he is above the law. In the two years I worked at a shelter for victims of domestic violence, none of the women for whom restraining orders were issued were directly physically or verbally threatened by their abusers, although each one feared reprisal. Also, it's likely to be the breakup itself, rather than the restraining order, that incites the threats or violence. "If you get a restraining order and he violates it, the police can arrest him. It is a legal document that spells out very clearly what he can't do to you and your family."

"I don't want him to be arrested. I just want him to leave us alone."

"I'm sure you don't want him arrested, but he isn't leaving your family alone and is now making threats to their safety. He sounds very unstable, and you don't have any reason to believe that he won't carry out his threats, do you?" They both shook their heads. "He doesn't have to be arrested. All he needs to do is comply with the provisions of the restraining order. That's really up to him."

Laura and her mother understood the severity of the boy's behavior and got the restraining order. He was notified and given a copy. It was difficult to enforce at school, and on several occasions he tried to bother her. She warned him that she would call the police if he didn't leave her alone. He told her that she was a scared bitch and she'd never do it. She called his bluff and telephoned the police from the principal's office. The police came to the school, which caused a scene and embarrassed him.

They let him off with a stern warning and told him that if he violated the order again, they would arrest him. He didn't bother Laura again but was delighted to show off his new girlfriend in front of her every chance he had. Laura wasn't jealous; she felt sorry for the girl.

14

Who Will Our Daughters Become?

What We Want for Girls in an Ideal World

HOW CAN YOU HELP your daughter become the most powerful and self-assured woman she can be? You want to ensure that she will never choose another abusive mate and will live a happier, more fulfilling life. Your daughter's abusive dating relationship has been a harrowing experience for the entire family, and you never want to repeat it again.

Throughout this book, you have specifically learned about teen dating violence. You can now recognize the different types of abuse, the red flags to look for in a potentially abusive relationship, the various causes of behavior in both your daughter and her boyfriend, and the role played by drugs and alcohol. You have honestly appraised your own family and taken personal responsibility where necessary. You have shown relevant material in this book to your daughter. By now, you may have taken decisive legal or medical action.

You may recall that in the introduction I stated that most of the women I worked with at the battered women's shelter had gone through several abusive relationships before they decided that enough was enough and got out. Unfortunately, they and their children suffered tremendous physical and emotional trauma before that decision was reached. In addition, statistically, most women leave each of their abusers five to seven times before they leave for good . . . if they're still alive. Because they did not learn what you have learned by reading this book, these women were destined to repeat their abusive relationships over and over again without knowing why. Lack of self-esteem is one of the main reasons women repeat this abusive pattern.

THE ROLE OF SELF-ESTEEM

Positive self-esteem is one of the most precious gifts we can give our children. It is better than a trip to Disney World, a PlayStation, or a two-wheeler. It is a parent's responsibility to tell and show her daughter that she is the finest creature on earth; that she is loved for the very fact of her being, not for her achievements; that she can be anything she would like to be; and that she has your full support. You may notice I said that parents must show as well as tell their daughter these things. Why? Because love is a behavior. Perhaps you don't know how to give this gift to your daughter because your parents never gave it to you. Is it possible that you don't feel as good about yourself as you would like? Maybe you have seen the consequences of low self-esteem in your own life and would like your daughter to experience better than you've had.

How a girl feels about herself crucially affects every part of her life: the way she functions at school, her female relationships, the way she feels she belongs—or doesn't—in her family, and how high in life she is likely to rise. In your household you have witnessed firsthand the way in which self-esteem has affected her choice of a boyfriend, as well as the length of time she allowed herself to stay in a negative and possibly dangerous relationship. You have seen the extent she has gone to in order to save an unhealthy relationship as well as the ways she allowed herself to be devastated at the hands of an abusive boyfriend. This is poor self-esteem in action.

Nathaniel Branden, known as the "father of self-esteem," states that, apart from problems that are biological in origin, he can't think of a single psychological difficulty that is not traceable to poor self-esteem: anxiety, depression, fear of intimacy or success, alcohol or drug abuse, underachievement at school or work, spousal abuse and child molestation, emotional immaturity, suicide, and crimes of violence.

Self-esteem has two parts: a feeling of personal competence and a feeling of personal worth. In other words, you can envision self-esteem as a math quotient in which self-confidence plus self-respect equals positive self-esteem. It reflects your daughter's judgment about her right to be happy. When your daughter has low self-esteem, she not only feels wrong about certain issues and challenges, she feels wrong as a person, and that she is somehow defective. She is plagued by feelings of inadequacy, insecurity, self-doubt, guilt, and a sense that she is not enough. Surely you can see the ways in which these fears were played out in her abusive relationship.

The higher your daughter's self-esteem, the more likely she is to form healthy rather than destructive relationships in the future, since health is attracted to health. Your daughter was initially plagued by poor self-esteem, which became lower the longer she stayed with her abusive boyfriend. Every time he called her a vulgar name, demeaned her, or physically or sexually violated her, it lowered her self-esteem further, thereby validating the feelings she already had about herself. As I mentioned in chapter 2, when a boy tells his girlfriend that she is "fat," "ugly," "lazy," "stupid," a "bitch," a "whore," and that "nobody would want her," the girl with high self-esteem would answer, "Then why are *you* with me?" When she has poor self-esteem, a girl thinks to herself, "He must be right. I am all of those things. I'd better stay with him because no one else would want me."

How can you nurture your daughter's self-esteem now? You can begin by telling her that you believe she can make good choices for herself and that you trust her to do so. Teach her to trust and respect herself and to solve her own problems. Let her know, by your actions, that you love and value her, and that your love will never be taken away from her, no matter what happens in her life. Most girls grow up learning to be professional people-pleasers. Let her make mistakes and learn from them. They aren't mistakes if a lesson was learned.

Her destructive relationship is a perfect opportunity. You can ask her what she learned about herself while in this relationship and how she looks at it now in hindsight. What could she have seen throughout the course of her time with her boyfriend that would have tipped her off that he was abusive? More important, what *instincts* did she have that she ignored because she feared losing him? I have found that women in abusive relationships had many subtle gut feelings all through the relationship and chose to look the other way rather than trusting themselves. Staying in their destructive relationship became more important than their own self-respect, emotional health and well-being, and physical safety.

In order for your daughter to become self-assured, she must accept complete responsibility for her own well-being and learn to take charge of her life as a future woman. High self-esteem means learning to accept herself as a valuable person, regardless of past mistakes. You must let her know that high esteem comes from liking who she *is*, rather than what she *has* or what she *does*. It is a lesson never learned by many adults, who define their personal worth by a bigger house, a better car, nicer clothes, a promotion, and so on. If this is the case in your lives, perhaps both you and your daughter can learn these lessons together, lifting each other's esteem as you go.

Look at the following questions, which are part of a self-esteem questionnaire. I have marked the responses that show high self-esteem *true*:

1. I usually feel inferior to others.
2. I normally feel warm and happy toward myself. *True*
3. I often feel adequate to handle new situations. *True*
4. I habitually condemn myself for my mistakes and shortcomings.
5. I am free of shame, blame, guilt, and remorse. *True*
6. I am very concerned about what others think and say of me.
7. I have a strong need for recognition and approval.
8. I usually anticipate new endeavors with quiet confidence. *True*
9. I normally do my own thinking and make my own decisions. *True*
10. I often defer to others.
11. I am free to give precedence to my own needs and desires. *True*
12. I tend to belittle my own talents and achievements.
13. I am free to speak up for my own opinions and convictions. *True*
14. I feel very vulnerable to others' opinions, comments, and attitudes.
15. I am fearful of exposing my "real self."
16. I am a compulsive perfectionist.
17. I rarely feel uncomfortable, lonely, and isolated when alone. *True*
18. I often avoid new endeavors because of a fear of mistakes or failure.

Taking this short quiz will help both you and your daughter clearly see the areas of self-esteem that she (and perhaps you) would like to improve upon. No one has perfect positive self-esteem all the time. Self-esteem is on a continuum, ebbing and flowing with situations in our lives. However, we want our daughters to have a core of benevolent feelings about themselves that cannot be easily shaken.

Last, if your family believes in a higher power, you can let her know that she is a child of God, a product of the universe, at one with all of nature. These entities give us a sense of belonging and self-worth.

I felt that I was lower than low, like I was a bug squished into the dirt. I was the "smart child" in the family and always expected to do well. My brother was the jock. If I got a B on a test, it was the end of the world in my house. If my brother missed a layup in a basketball game, it was "He threw you a bad pass. You're a better player than any of your teammates, son." I really tried hard to please my parents and be the perfect kid. I felt like I was only worth anything as a person when I was doing exactly what they expected of me.

When I had my first boyfriend at sixteen, he was very nice and gave me a lot of compliments. It wasn't all about how smart I was, but that I was pretty, funny, and sexy. At first I didn't believe him, but after about three months of this nice treatment, I fell in love with him. I loved that attention, and for the first time in my life, I felt like I was loved.

When he started calling me names, like "idiot," "moron," or "crazy," it was like I was back home, and I figured that he must have found out who I really was. It got worse and worse, until I was almost unable to get out of bed in the morning. I was so depressed. Here he looked like someone who was going to care about me, rather than what I had to achieve, but I was wrong. He was just like my parents.

I went to see the school counselor because I couldn't concentrate and my grades were slipping. I was afraid to tell my parents. She had just put together a group of other students who she felt could do some work on their self-esteem. That group saved my life. I didn't feel like I was alone or that I was crazy. We did a lot of painful work on our feelings about ourselves, and why we felt that way. I became closer to those people than my own family. After about a month, I was able to leave my boyfriend because I didn't feel like he was good enough for me. After another month, I could tell my parents that I thought I was good enough just the way I was and I was doing the best I could.

Having better self-esteem changed all of my relationships—with other people and with myself. After talking to my counselor, my parents decided to get into therapy for themselves and with me, which really surprised me. I never would have thought they'd be open to that. It was a hard thing for them to do, but the results were great.

Today I'm going to a good college and have a very sweet boyfriend. It took me a long time to trust him, and maybe I'm still on guard a little, which I think is fine. I still have rough days like everyone else, and I have a tendency to try to be the best at everything or to blame myself for things I didn't even do. I have to stop, slow down, and remind myself that I'm only human, and a pretty good human. Improving my self-esteem improved every part of my life.

—KAREN, NINETEEN

HEALTHY DATING RELATIONSHIPS

You have been through a terrible experience with your daughter's abusive boyfriend. No one would blame you if you scrutinized every other boy she brought home in the future. In order to help her make better choices in future dating relationships, it is important to teach her what a good one looks like.

In their book *Making Life Choices*, Frances Sizer, Eleanor Whitney, and Linda DeBryne explain the characteristics of a healthy relationship: "First, each partner in a relationship must have a positive self-image. Once you feel strong and sure of yourself, you are better able to know what to look for in a partner. Second, you should be aware, always, that love develops in stages . . . and cannot be rushed. Once you find an appropriate partner, do not give in to the temptation to try to 'hurry things along' by skipping early phases of development. These early times provide the foundation of a strong relationship later on. Be patient."

The authors explain the stages that go into building a healthy relationship. I believe it would be wise to show them to your daughter. Ask her to think about the stages she missed or rushed through in her relationship with her boyfriend. Then ask her why she thinks she did that; what was going on in her mind? These stages are

Stage 1: attraction

Something about the person catches your attention. You are attracted to each other.

Stage 2: casual friendship

You and a person who interests you enjoy activities together. For example, you both may enjoy movies or ball games, and plan those activities together. During this stage, you explore each other's characteristics. Each is on "best behavior," so commitments are not yet appropriate.

Stage 3: close friendship

As you spend more time together, you learn about each other's feelings and values. You begin to discover each other's emotional and spiritual tendencies. At this stage the relationship may progress or retreat.

Stage 4: intimate friendship

The friends reveal their faults. They let down their masks of best behavior, and reality sets in. By this time each trusts the other's acceptance, because the true self of each—complete with faults—has been seen by the other. The couple may decide to go steady or may relax back to being close friends.

Stage 5: mature love

In this stage, all the initial hurdles are past. Each partner continues developing socially, intellectually, emotionally, and spiritually. The degree of closeness in mature love makes conflict likely, but the partners learn to resolve conflict in healthy ways.

I was in such a hurry to snag him. All my girlfriends said he was so great and I was so lucky that he was even looking in my direction. I wanted to get serious with him real fast before he found someone else. —REBECCA, FIFTEEN

In *Making Life Choices*, the authors relate important qualities that teens (and everyone) should look for in a partner. A prospective partner

- is not involved in other love relationships.
- is well over heartaches; has not just recently broken up with someone else.
- is open to being in a relationship with you.
- is free of chemical or psychological addictions. (People with addictions to alcohol or other drugs, people who gamble, or people with eating disorders cannot function well in love relationships.)
- has time to devote to a relationship.
- has high self-esteem.
- is close to you geographically—lives in your city or state.
- is compatible with you in terms of social values and beliefs.
- has several close friends.
- is a person you would still want as a friend if the love relationship ended.
- treats others well, even if they are strangers.

These lists, along with the Teen Relationship Equality Wheel in chapter 2, will help your daughter define what she truly wants in her next relationship.

In my private practice I see many women in their thirties and forties who have experienced unsatisfying relationships with men. They desperately want to find a healthy relationship and perhaps get married. They tell me, "There aren't any good men out there," "All men are weird," or "It's hopeless. I'll never find a mate." More often than not, they haven't clearly defined what they are looking for in a partner.

I suggest to them that they go home and write down all the qualities they would like in a man. It can be anything: a certain height, weight, level of education, or family background, as well as certain qualities of character. No one else will look at the list, so no one will judge it. This list may be as long as they wish. Then I ask them to look at that list and narrow it down to ten to fifteen characteristics on which they *will not compromise*. These usually (or hopefully) tend to be things like honesty in all areas of his life, a good feeling about women, fidelity, dependability, loyalty, caring, and so on.

I encourage these patients to become everything on their list that they desire in a mate. In other words, become their own perfect partner. In that way, they not only fully understand what those characteristics are, but they will not look for a man to fill something in them that they don't already have.

I suggest that you try this exercise with your daughter. If she doesn't care to, she doesn't need to show you her list. Remind her to think carefully about the characteristics on the list because she is agreeing that she will not compromise on anything less. Ask her if she is all the things she requires in a boyfriend. I find that when people are asked to actually define what they are looking for, they understand themselves more fully. The difficult part of this exercise, for them, is requiring them to be that person first.

> *I never knew what I was looking for in a guy. I just figured I'd know when I met him. Obviously, I was wrong about that, because I thought my last boyfriend was Mr. Right and he was Mr. Wrong.*
> —PERI, SEVENTEEN

EFFECTIVE COMMUNICATION SKILLS

It is so important for our daughters to learn to talk with everyone in their lives more clearly and effectively. No doubt your daughter was upset about the way her boyfriend treated her but was too afraid to speak up for herself or simply didn't know how. Certainly, no one likes to be called a "bitch," or the other horrible names he said to her. No one enjoys being pushed or slapped, but in your daughter's case, she probably didn't say anything about it. I'd like to share with you some tips for more effective communication.

There are four different styles of communicating we use when talking with others. The first style is *passive*. The passive person doesn't ask for what she wants and expects others to read her mind in order to find out what she wants. When that doesn't happen, she may sulk or silently feel upset. She can't say no effectively but then feels like others are walking all over her. She may apologize for what she says, or blame herself when things go wrong.

The *aggressive* communicator speaks loudly and uses violent words in order to get what he wants. He acts overbearing and intimidating. It may be difficult for him to express his feelings except through anger. He blames others when things go wrong and frequently gets his needs met at the expense of others.

The *passive-aggressive* person seems to have a motto: Don't get mad, get even. She doesn't ask for the things she wants and frequently feels stepped on. She retaliates by making a silent, though vicious, attack. This may be in the form of inaction, back-stabbing, gossip, and so on. But she never directly confronts the person she feels has harmed her.

The *assertive* person communicates feelings and opinions clearly and directly. She speaks in a confident voice that can be easily heard and uses eye contact. She can say no when she feels it is necessary and can accept it from others. She takes responsibility for her own actions. Because she is so clear in her statements, she is able to get her needs met without harming herself or others.

Usually a person will have one communication style that predominates, but sometimes a girl will use a passive style with her boyfriend but be quite assertive with her parents. It is important to pay close attention to how your daughter communicates in different situations.

Ask your daughter what kind of communicator she was in her

abusive relationship and why. What kind of communicator was her boyfriend? How did she feel when he used that style of speaking with her? Naturally, you would like your daughter to be assertive. You can help her practice these skills. Here are two ways.

First, ask her to do something for you. She should answer, "Let me think about that and get back to you." She is not saying yes reflexively.

Second, ask her to do something else and have her answer, "No, I can't do that now. Maybe some other time." Notice that she doesn't say, "I'm sorry, but I can't do that now." There is no need for her to feel sorry and, therefore, guilty. She is stating her opinion and standing up for herself. Have her speak clearly and look you directly in the eyes.

Do these exercises several times. Tell her how much more assertive and direct she sounds, and how you respect her feelings so much more than you had. She sounds kind and thoughtful in her replies, though not like someone who can be pushed around.

> I was such a wuss whenever I talked to my boyfriend. I didn't want to upset him or for him to think that I was demanding. He told me that his last girlfriend was really demanding and controlling. I was afraid to tell him my opinions and feelings about almost anything if they didn't agree with his. Then I'd get mad and silently blow up because I felt like he didn't care.
>
> —NICKI, SIXTEEN

> I never knew what a good dating relationship was supposed to be like. I never knew that I had a say in what happened on a date. I just figured you sort of go along until something feels bad.
>
> —ANGELA, SEVENTEEN

A RELATIONSHIP CONTRACT

I think it is crucial for every girl to have a clear understanding of what she would like in a relationship—the behaviors she expects of herself and her boyfriend. Most often, girls don't think about what *they* would like when dating. They are usually trying to please their boyfriends so they will stick around. The following list is extrapolated from a relationship contract put together by Interface Children and Family Services. Ask your daughter to answer these questions:

DATING

1. Should every weekend and evening be spent with your boyfriend?
2. Who decides what to do and where to go on a date?
3. What about expenses? Should the boy always be expected to pay?
4. If your date always pays for expenses, are you obligated to go along with his sexual advances?
5. How much do you want you or your date to use alcohol or other drugs?
6. Is there any situation in which it would be okay for your date to push you around? To hit you?

SEXUAL RIGHTS

1. Are you free to say that you do or don't want to go any further sexually?
2. At what point may a person refuse to have sex?
3. If you and your boyfriend agree to have intercourse, whose responsibility is it to use birth control? To protect against AIDS and other sexually transmitted diseases?

OTHER RELATIONSHIPS

1. Are you and your boyfriend free to make friendships with other people? If so, how will you deal with jealousy?
2. Is it all right for both you and your boyfriend to make friends with people of the opposite sex?
3. Do you include each other in those relationships?

PRIORITIES

1. What do you consider the most important ingredients in a relationship?
2. What qualities are most important to you in a boyfriend?

HOW YOUR DAUGHTER CAN PROTECT HERSELF

One of the ways your daughter can prevent future abusive relationships is to be very clear with the boys she comes into contact with. When she learns to communicate assertively, it will be easier. The following ideas will help her.

- Stay away from boys who put you down a lot, talk negatively about women, or drink and/or use drugs.
- Don't get involved with a boy who doesn't ask for your opinion or doesn't respect you or your decisions.
- Set sexual limits and communicate them clearly. Most teenage boys say, "I'll go as far as the girl will let me."
- Stay sober in social situations.
- Don't make boys guess what you want—tell them.
- When on a date, remain in control. Have an alternate transportation plan in case the date isn't going as you

would like and you want to go home. Do not rely on your date to bring you home.

- Listen to and trust your feelings and instincts.
- As soon as you feel threatened, forget about being a "nice girl."
- Take care of yourself. Don't assume someone else will.
- If a boy tries to use physical force and you must defend yourself, do not hit him in the stomach, shoulders, or back. These are the strongest parts of the human body. Target the kneecaps, heels, eyes, or crotch. If possible, do not stay and fight. Flee! You have fifteen minutes of an adrenaline surge, which will give you energy and extraordinary strength. Use it to run, get help, and yell, "Call 911!"

I hope this chapter has helped you better define what you would like for your daughter in a perfect world and the ways that you can help her achieve these things. Remember, the entire world need not be perfect, just her little corner.

By using the tools discussed here, you have performed a wonderful act for your daughter: you have taught her to feel confident and good about herself. You have helped her define what she wants for herself in future relationships. You have let your daughter see that she can speak in a way that others will hear and define her rights in a relationship with a boy who deserves her. Congratulations on all your hard work. I hope you have learned not only how to extricate your daughter from her abusive relationship but a few things about yourself as well, and new ways to improve your family in general.

I wish you all a happy and healthy future together.

Resources

Throughout this book I have shown you the causes of abusive teen dating relationships and some steps you can take now to help extricate your daughter from such a relationship. The following books, support groups, and organizations can lead you the rest of the way. Every hot line and organization listed here will allow you to remain anonymous.

I have not included referrals for services that offer psychological counseling because the choice of a therapist is very personal. However, the Domestic Violence Hotline listed below can refer you to therapists in your area who specialize in teen violence. Rest assured, there is counseling available to those in every income bracket. Refer to your yellow pages for low-cost counseling centers in your area.

Additional counseling services may be available to you through your place of worship and usually incorporate a spiritual component. The YWCA, the Boys and Girls Clubs, or any of their affiliated organizaions are also good resources for therapeutic services and referrals in your town.

You may consider asking your daughter's school counselor if there are support groups for girls in abusive dating relationships. There is such a need that many schools have started offering such groups.

Also consider whether your daughter would benefit from a self-defense class or martial arts training. Although she may never use the physical skills learned, many girls report that they feel more empowered and confident after taking these classes. The YWCA, YMCA, and Boys and Girls Clubs in your town may also be of help in this area. Martial arts headings are listed in the yellow pages.

Finally, consult the front of your telephone directory for a listing of community services in your area in every category.

DATING VIOLENCE AND DOMESTIC VIOLENCE

Books

Betancourt, Marian. *What to Do When Love Turns Violent: A Practical Resource for Women in Abusive Relationships*. New York: HarperCollins, 1997. Vital information on getting safe, getting help, and getting away. Praised by Oprah and the *New York Times* as "the best single resource."

Cardarelli, Albert. *Violence Between Intimate Partners: Patterns, Causes, Consequences, and Solutions*. New York: Prentice-Hall, 1969. Explains the causes and effects of violence, including policy issues, the role of law enforcement, social services, and the courts. For adults.

Hicks, John. *Dating Violence: True Stories of Hurt and Hope*. Brookfield, Conn.: Millbrook, 1996. Follows a first-person account of a 15-year-old girl through her physically, emotionally, and sexually abusive relationship. The author also analyzes dating patterns and relationships in general. For teens.

Johnson, Scott. *When "I Love You" Turns Violent: Abuse in Dating Relationships*. New York: New Horizons, 1993. Discusses early danger signs. For all ages.

Levy, Barrie. *Dating Violence: Young Women in Danger*. Seattle: Seal Press, 1998. A cross-cultural view of dating violence with first-person accounts. For all ages.

———. *In Love and in Danger: A Teen's Guide to Breaking Free of Abusive Relationships*. Seattle: Seal Press, 1998. How to identify an abusive relationship and facts about dating violence. For teens.

———. *What Parents Need to Know About Dating Violence: Learning the Facts and Helping Your Teen*. Seattle: Seal Press, 1995. Offers information, advice, and real-life stories about abusive relationships from parents and teens. For adults.

McShane, Claudette. *Warning: Dating May Be Hazardous to Your Health!* Mother Courage, 1989. Warning signs of an abusive relationship and tips for avoiding a bad relationship. For teens.

Pirog-Good, Maureen, and Jan Stets. *Violence in Dating Relationships*. Westport, Conn.: Praeger, 1989. A scholarly book that examines teen dating violence. For adults.

Rue, Nancy. *Everything You Need to Know About Abusive Relationships*. New York: Rosen, 1998. Offers teens a breadth of knowledge about dating violence.

Wartski, Maureen. *If You Leave Me.* Juniper Press, 1997. A fictional account of an abusive relationship from a teenage girl's point of view. For teens.

Internet

Keyword: domestic violence. Many links to information, support groups, books, and organizations specializing in domestic and dating violence.

Organizations

National Domestic Violence Hotline: 800-799-SAFE. A 24-hour referral service for domestic-violence shelters and therapists specializing in the treatment of abusive relationships.

Teen Line: 800-852-8336 (9:00 P.M. to 1:00 A.M. Eastern Standard Time, 6:00 to 10:00 P.M. Pacific Standard Time). An anonymous forum for teens to talk with a counselor.

EMOTIONAL WELL-BEING

Books

Cytryn, Leon, M.D., and Donald McKnew, M.D. *Growing Up Sad: Childhood Depression and Treatment.* New York: W. W. Norton, 1998. Examines the symptoms of depression at various ages in childhood, including diagnosis and treatment options. For adults.

Vanzant, Iyanla. *In the Meantime.* New York: Simon and Schuster, 1998. A prescription for how to be happy at the place you are in your life now, and happier in the future. For all ages.

Internet

Keywords: depression; mental health. Many opportunities to find organizations, literature, and support groups specializing in emotional well-being. Also, listings for post-traumatic stress disorder support groups and treatment.

LEGAL SERVICES

Organizations

Break the Cycle: 888-988-TEEN (11:30 A.M. to 8:30 P.M. Eastern Standard Time, 8:30 A.M. to 5:30 P.M. Pacific Standard Time), or www.breakthe-cycle.com. Advises teens and their parents about their legal rights in abusive relationships.

Victims of Crime Resource Center: 800-842-8467. Provides 24-hour legal information and referrals nationwide.

MISSING CHILDREN AND RUNAWAYS

Organizations

Child Quest International: 888-818-4673 (24 hours)

National Center for Missing and Exploited Children: 800-843-5678 (24 hours)

Polly Klaas Foundation: 800-587-4357 (24 hours)

All three organizations listed above provide assistance in locating missing children.

Covenant House: 800-999-9999 (24 hours). A shelter for 18- to 21-year-olds that provides housing, food, schooling, and job training. Residents may bring their children. Locations in New York, New Jersey, Texas, Florida, California, Michigan, Pennsylvania, Alaska, Washington, D.C., Louisiana, and Toronto.

Internet

Keyword: missing children

SELF-ESTEEM

Books

Branden, Nathaniel. *How to Raise Your Self-Esteem*. New York: Bantam, 1988.

————. *The Six Pillars of Self-Esteem*. New York: Bantam, 1995.

In both books the "father of self-esteem" offers step-by-step techniques for developing and strengthening feelings of self-worth. For all ages.

Sanford, Linda, and Mary Ellen Donovan. *Women and Self-Esteem*. New York: Viking, 1985. Explains the way in which women's harmful attitudes about themselves are shaped and offers exercises to build self-esteem. For all ages.

Internet

Keyword: self-esteem. Offers literature about self-esteem development and self-improvement, as well as workshops and books.

SEX AND FAMILY PLANNING

Books

Bell, Ruth. *Changing Bodies, Changing Lives: A Book for Teens in Sex and Relationships*. New York: Times Books, 1998. A discussion of sex, physical and emotional health, and relationships. For teens.

Boston Health Book Collective. *Our Bodies, Ourselves for the New Century: A Book by and for Women.* New York: Touchstone, 1998. An updated version of the book that teaches everything you ever wanted to know about sex, health, and relationships. For all ages.

Moglia, Ronald, and John Knowles. *All About Sex: A Family Resource on Sex and Sexuality.* New York: Crown, 1997. The latest information on every aspect of sex and sexuality. For all ages.

Pinsky, Drew, M.D., and Adam Carolla. *Dr. Drew and Adam Handbook: A Survival Guide to Life and Love.* New York: Dell, 1998. Straight talk about love and sex. For teens.

Vitkus, Jessica, and Jessica Weeks Ingall. *Smart Sex.* New York: Pocket, 1998. A hip, insightful book on teenage sexuality and sexual choices. For teens.

Organizations

Planned Parenthood: 800-239-PLAN (24 hours). Comprehensive family planning and birth control, including testing and treatment for STD's.

SEXUAL ASSAULT AND SEXUALLY TRANSMITTED DISEASES

Books

Shuker-Haines, Frances. *Everything You Need to Know About Date Rape.* New York: Rosen, 1995. Offers information, resources, and hope to victims of sexual assault. For teens.

Organizations

Centers for Disease Control and Prevention: 800-227-8922 (24 hours). Hot line for information on sexually transmitted diseases.

Rape Crisis Hotline: 800-656-HOPE (24 hours). Referrals for treatment across the nation, as well as victim witness services.

U.S. Department of Health and Human Services: 800-336-4797 (24 hours). Information and referrals to national resources.

SUBSTANCE ABUSE

Books

Althauser, Doug. *You Can Free Yourself from Alcohol and Drugs.* Oakland, Calif.: New Harbinger, 1998. A ten-goal approach to recovery focusing on lifestyle changes rather than the spiritual transformation of the traditional twelve-step approach. For all ages.

Heuer, Marti. *Teen Addiction*. New York: Ballantine, 1995. Goes through the steps of helping an addicted teen. For adults.

Kuhn, Cynthia, Scott Swartzwelder, and Wilkie Wilson. *Buzzed*. New York: W. W. Norton, 1998. Lists all types of drugs, their slang names and effects.

Mass, Wendy. *Teen Drug Abuse*. San Diego, Calif.: Lucent, 1998. Discusses various drugs used by teens: why they are used, consequences, treatment, and prevention. For all ages.

McLaughlin, Miriam Smith. *Addiction: The "High" That Brings You Down*. Springfield, N.J.: Enslow, 1997. Describes the various types of drug addictions and their symptoms. For teens.

Milan, James, M.D., and Katherine Ketcham. *Under the Influence*. New York: Bantam, 1993. Examines the physical factors that set alcoholics and nonalcoholics apart, and new ways of treating alcoholism. For adults.

Stewart, Gail, and Carl Franzen. *Teen Addicts*. San Diego, Calif.: Lucent, 1999. Discusses the signs and symptoms of teen addiction. For all ages.

Strack, Jay. *Drugs and Drinking: What Every Teen and Parent Should Know*. Nashville: Thomas Nelson, 1985. Describes various drugs and the consequences of alcohol consumption by teens. For all ages.

Watson, Arnold. *Cocaine Addiction*. New York: W. W. Norton, 1991. Treatment, recovery, and relapse prevention of cocaine addiction. For adults.

Organizations

Alcoholics Anonymous World Services: 888-425-2666 (24 hours). Referrals to AA, Al-Anon, and Alateen meetings in your town. Also, referrals to "Young People's" AA meetings.

American Self-Help Clearinghouse: 973-625-7101 (Hours may vary). Has state-by-state listings of several hundred self-help organizations.

Center for Substance Abuse and Treatment: 800-662-HELP (24 hours). Referral routing service to appropriate help in your area.

Cocaine Anonymous: 800-347-8998 (24 hours). Provides information and referrals.

Narcotics Anonymous: 818-773-9999 (24 hours). Referrals for meetings in your area.

Internet

Keywords: substance abuse, Alcoholics Anonymous. Provide links to agencies specializing in substance-abuse treatment, as well as information and literature.

Index